GROWING AND ARRANGING
CHURCH FLOWERS
FOR SEASONAL
AND
SPECIAL OCCASIONS

D1458849

By the same author:

THE MINIATURE FLOWER ARRANGEMENT BOOK

Growing and Arranging
CHURCH FLOWERS
for Seasonal
and
Special Occasions

by

MARGARET BEST

photographs by

GODFREY BEST, A.I.I.P.

MOWBRAY
LONDON & OXFORD

ISBN 0–264–66888–X (hardback)
ISBN 0–264–66845–6 (paperback)

First published 1982
by A. R. Mowbray & Co. Ltd.
Saint Thomas House, Becket Street,
Oxford, OX1 1SJ

Typeset by Cotswold Typesetting Ltd., Gloucester and
Printed in Great Britain by Cambridge University Press

Contents

(Sixteen pages of Colour plates are between pp 80 and 81)

5

Preface

Church Flowers for Seasonal and Special occasions; this title immediately brings to my mind colour. It is one of the most important subjects of our lives, and in terms of church decoration the background, the foreground, the hangings, the altar frontals, the woodwork, the vestments and perhaps the chairs or pews influence our minds in terms of colour. The windows are always my next concern, how much clear daylight will I have for a certain occasion and how the stained glass will affect the colourings of the flowers when artificial light is added.

Whether the special occasion is to be for youth or age, or perhaps somewhere in the middle, whether it is for a church festival of Easter, Whitsun or Christmas, whether the church is minute, holding less than fifty people, or it is of parish size or cathedral size, I see it in the terms of colour for the special occasion.

My first initiation to church flowers was when I was about four years old being taken by my mother to help decorate the pulpit in our parish church as this was our allotted place. It was an open-work wooden structure—of late Victorian design. This presented no particular difficulties as the lower part was arranged with indoor ferns, and the upper part arranged in cones, shaped metal containers, tied to the upper struts, they were filled with water, the foliage added with the flowers arranged into and between the stems. From that time onwards as amateur and professional it has been my privilege and great pleasure to arrange flowers in many small country churches, medium sized suburban ones, city churches and vast cathedrals for special occasions.

Readers will realise that a number of the individual groups were photographed under studio conditions in order to achieve greater definition.

M.B.

Introduction

Since the very early days, from pre Christian times it has been customary practice to decorate all places of worship with branches of trees and sweet smelling herbs. The reasons for doing this were many, to ward off evil spirits with magical powers, to charm with beauty and elegance, and last but not least to improve the general aroma.

Garlands and decorations first came into our homes as a protection against the powers of evil. For the Romans, holly was a symbol of peace and goodwill and so later came to be used in our churches. Up to 1850 the sexton would hang branches of holly around the church. According to a record in the St Albans Times of 1883, 'the lady flower arrangers brought an artistic touch to the decorations of the Abbey.' So, therefore, flowers were introduced more liberally into the Christmas decorations between 1850 and 1883. Another remnant of sun worship is the Christmas tree, which shows the power of the sun to cover the world with green.

Many of our indigenous evergreen trees and shrubs were used for the beautification of our early churches and it can be seen from the very early drawings, sketches and woodcuts that such foliage as holly, ivy, laurel, box and yew, evergreen oak, conifers and mistletoe were used for this purpose. As the years passed by, such evergreen herbs were introduced as their special qualities were discovered and appreciated. Rosemary and lavender and other aromatic herbs were found to be extremely useful and decorative.

The mistletoe is especially interesting since it was intimately connected with many superstitions of the ancient British and Germans. The Celts and Druids held the mistletoe in great esteem for its magical virtues. Latterly Nicholas Culpeper 1616–1654 styled it as an 'all-heal' and as an antidote for all diseases, which brings us to the present days, where mistletoe and all the other foliages are still used for decoration throughout the country, a surviving custom of the British Christmas festival.

Nowadays many places of worship are lavishly decorated throughout the year, for the beautification of the building and to the Glory of God.

Church Festivals known to all Christians are recognised throughout the year, passing from Advent to Christmas and to Easter— progressing as they do year after year through the Church Calendar— sometimes adhering to the old established liturgical colours, in the colours of their flowers. Special sacraments of the Church, such as Baptism and Holy Matrimony call for individual colouring, blending colours of altar frontals and hangings and vestments with the flower

9

arrangements for the decoration of the Church and for such a special occasion for the bride, her personal flowers and those of the bridesmaids.

During the last decade and a half something quite new has evolved in the history of the church, namely The Flower Festival, where thousands of talented and faithful flower arrangers have given their time and their hands to beautifying their church and cathedral with simple garden and exotic flowers, for the dual purpose of raising funds to restore ancient buildings and for charities and to give great pleasure to all.

The flower arrangements in the English Churches shown in this book have been exclusively arranged by myself (with one or two exceptions) for Special Occasions and in June 1980 I had the honour of being invited to arrange the decoration for the Bishops Throne for the Enthronement of the Bishop of St Albans, the Rt Revd John B. Taylor.

Decorating for Special Occasions requires a great deal of fore-thought. I always like to have my flowers a day or two ahead of the occasion so that I can have them in perfect condition. So many flowers like gladioli, lilies and even roses need to have special treatment. By putting them in warm water in a light window I can bring them on to peak development; likewise the only flowers in a particular colour are already rather advanced, then they have to have their development arrested. Having cut them and split the stems where necessary I place them in cold water, wrapped in newspaper, in the coldest possible place with paper over their heads in order to keep them in the dark, there they remain for 24–48 hours totally static, and ready for the appointed hour of the special occasion.

The most generally useful hint, I think, is this. In arranging mixed flowers, try to use whatever comes to hand. Any one with a garden however small can produce a mixture of flowers and leaves. These in turn can be arranged with feeling, with a sense of line and colour and even of drama, if this is achieved with character and quality, then they have really created something unique.

When arranging flowers or branches of one kind it is a good plan to try to recapture in your arrangement something of the essential quality of the subject and its special way of growing. A good example of this is the arrangement of magnolia and arum lilies on p. 57 (also see colour plate 3) and the wild sloe in the bronze vase on p. 52. Not only is one admiring the qualities of the flowers and leaves, but the shapes of the spaces, the voids which are an essential part of an arrangement.

I am always asked in which order do I make my arrangement. There is really no rule about this. I find I work as the mood takes me. However, as a leaf to me is as important as a flower, they go not always

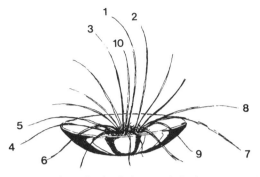

Suggestion for placing stems in bowl.

where I want them, but where they look most comfortable, in fact at the angle at which they were growing, so they go in in any order. When I use branches of foliage or blossom, they then go into the arrangement first, at the top and sides. I then place my tallest flowers gradually down through the group, using bigger flowers nearer the centre in order to draw the eye towards this centre, from which every stem radiates.

It is rather outdated now to have a background of green foliage placed in the vase first, with one or two exceptions. Where I had my extraordinarily difficult church to decorate, where the walls were covered with coloured mosaic tiles in very busy patterns, I then resorted to the old and only way of displaying the flowers. I used a background of foliage of laurel, carefully polished, and where too thickly covered in leaves I clipped away every other leaf to make the whole branch lighter in weight. The Arum lilies, weight for weight, teamed up very favourably with the laurel and showed up well against the very difficult background.

One wonders as one progresses through life how it is possible to avoid repeating or copying something that has been said or done before. Thankfully we are all individuals and although we may have a definite bias to a style in a certain form of art, no two works of art are the same. This is certainly true of painting, photography, and floral arrangments as examples.

I, like my professional colleagues know only too well how difficult it is to make a matching pair of flower arrangements, whether they be small, medium or large, which gives us our proof that every arrangement is unique. Repetition, there has to be, to serve the needs of newcomers to this wonderful world of flowers. They all want to know the basic principles of flower arrangement in the Western

World. Which flowers and foliages make harmonious groups and what dried materials look well together for the winter arrangement, and most important point of all, how to prolong the life of every leaf and flower.

After many weeks of quite ordinary practice of cutting and arranging available material, one becomes more aware of colours, shapes and textures of the subjects to use and of surrounding furniture and furnishings and the all important colour and texture of containers.

So many people nowadays enjoy growing their own 'little bits' so whether the garden is large or very small there are many worthwhile plants to recommend for cultivation.

All these points will be dealt with later in the book. The opportunities for learning the art of flower arrangement have become wider and wider as the demand grows. On an amateur basis one can learn from experience of trial and error by entering the classes for arrangements in the local flower show, the study of books and visiting neighbouring shows to criticize and admire. Evening classes at technical colleges can fill the needs of business people and the National Association of Flower Arrangement Societies can be a help, guide and inspiration to all would be arrangers. By becoming a member of the Association, for a small annual subscription, it is possible to attend a monthly demonstration in one's own town and by entering in simple competitions becoming more and more able to enjoy this splendid past-time. Now, with a good sound background so much pleasure can be had by viewing and taking part in projects large and small, traditional and contemporary. After a certain amount of tuition and a great deal of practice one becomes aware of outlines and shape, two important points which are not readily appreciated at first.

Working throughout the year in Great Britain, one passes through the four seasons and becomes aware of flowers and foliage in their own season and the experienced eye can tell at a glance when a certain bloom or leaf is mature and right for cutting.

One can always rely on the supply of flowers which are out of season as so many are now flown in from overseas, but it is always a delight to be able to use material grown, selected and cut by one's own hands for the specific time of year.

Assessing Architectural background

Every Church has its own particular characteristics—never have I found two even remotely alike.

The porches vary tremendously, so too do the pillars, the aisles, the font, the pulpit and lectern, the chancel with its various styles of choir stall, the sanctuary, the altar rails, the altar itself, the reredos and the windows, whether they be clear glass or stained and leaded glass.

Some of the country churches built in the twelfth and thirteenth centuries are of local stone, the exterior and interior alike. These present few problems as the background colour is a delightful grey or warm pink toned sandstone— excellent colours for the background for flowers.

The tastes of parishes vary very much as some prefer their church interior to be whitewashed throughout, others prefer the colour of the natural stone and those who have inherited a Victorian or Edwardian place of worship, the red brick dominates the interior.

The Church I found most difficult to decorate with flowers was exactly that, red brick walls, the apse tiled to shoulder height in what one can only describe as an extremely busy pattern of mosaic—above that in bold type was inscribed the Ten Commandments. The answer to this problem will be discussed later.

On offering or being invited to help decorate a place of worship I cannot recommend too strongly that one should first visit the church, walk about, sit in different places, assess the natural lighting, the artifical lighting, the size of the windows and height from the ground and in fact get the feeling of the place, the atmosphere, and overall colour and size.

As a general rule for flowers in church, simplicity is the keynote, for large buildings 'think big' and concentrate mainly on bold designs— with bold foliage and flowers, resist the temptation to use small flowers and concentrate on line and colour. Never cover a beautifully carved piece of church furniture, leave it free to be admired, placing a really good and well arranged group of flowers nearby.

Contemporary containers in white
and cream earthenware.
Good solid practical containers,
which hold plenty of water.

14

Two earthenware pitchers.
Stone coloured body, with ochre glazing on
the neck. Made at the Verwood Potteries
in the South of England.
The larger of the two is thirteen inches, the
smaller is nine inches.

15

Requirements for Church Decoration

Today there is the most wonderful selection of containers, pedestals and plinths from which to choose, but the most important item is a pair of stub scissors, purchased from your local florist. You really cannot live without them. They are made of top quality steel—they not only cut your flowers and foliage but your wire netting too.

For your church cupboard I recommend a good selection of vases bowls, troughs, jardinières, copies of Georgian wine coolers in lead—earthenware, fibre glass and plastic, and should the latter offend you—in bright plastic white—ponder on the thought that it is easy to carry and the vessel can be transformed by painting it with two thirds flat black paint with the addition of one third silver paint—so giving it a leaden appearance.

Other useful items include: dust sheets for clearing old arrangements and using for the new arrangement.

A roll of two inch wire netting, an invaluable commodity.

Blocks of Oasis—the green water absorbent material.

Watering cans, and Hand sprays.

Tubes or cones and canes for adding extra height to a particular stem.

Sellotape.

Florists wires for mending a damaged but precious stem.

Binding wire and string.

Polythene bags—in which to place a whole root of a plant, and in which to place a water saturated piece of oasis.

An absorbent cloth for mopping up afterwards.

Long broom.

Dust pan and brush. Steps and a ladder.

A board placed in a prominent position for a rota for the years decorations.

A list of dedicated and keen ladies who enjoy doing the flowers and even more dedicated person who can direct the arrangements throughout the year and is also able to buy well the best and longest lasting flowers at the lowest price.

The Care and Handling of Flowers and Foliage

The preparation of material, the selecting, cutting and conditioning is an extremely important part of flower arrangement.

If one can develop the vision that is necessary for selecting shapes of branches and stems to be used in a certain setting then the shape of the arrangement is sure to be natural looking, with the all essential quality of movement.

The time of day that one cuts material from the garden or hedgerow is most important, during the summer months, first thing in the morning or the cool of the evening are the best times.

Most flowers and branches can be divided into soft and hard stems, the former which includes all the narcissi family, tulips, alstroemeria and lilies and many, many more—need merely a slanting cut with an hour or two in deep cold water in a cool place. The latter, the hard stemmed subjects need to be split for an inch or two or hammered to crush the end of the stem so that water can be easily taken up. Examples of this type of stem include roses, chrysanthemums, stock, wallflowers, flowering shrubs and branches of trees, flowering and otherwise. It is always advisable to remove the thorns and lower leaves from roses, in fact remove all foliage that will be below the water-line as it is not only superfluous but it can soon foul the water.

The woody stems of philadelphus, lilac and guelder rose (viburnum) not only need their stems to be split, but the leaves surrounding the flowers should be removed to reduce transpiration and therefore assist the flowers in lasting longer.

There are several methods of prolonging the life of flowers, by warm water for reviving drooping flower heads, by boiling the tip of the stem for a few seconds, such as herbaceous campanula and all the spurges (euphorbia) and by plunging into deep cold water. Iced water will arrest the development of roses, if they are especially needed for a day or two hence. Arum lily leaves can be totally submerged in cold water overnight and hydrangea heads for an hour or two. Hollow stems can be supplied with extra water by up-ending the delphinium or lupin, filling the stem with water and plugging the end with cotton wool. The stem ends of poppies can be burnt over a flame for seconds only, then plunged into deep cold water. Finally the general condition of the arrangement can be maintained for a few extra days by adding sugar to the water—as a food, charcoal or antiseptic to keep it clean or by using a plant food dissolved in the water in the form of a white powder called Chrysal, easily obtained from the florist or garden centre.

1
Growing Shrubs

Such is the diversity of shrubs, that a garden can be almost entirely planted with them, the changing scene from flower to berry, the early scents and the late berries, with the thrilling colours of autumn they can be enjoyed during every month of the year. Lovely to look at and so useful for picking.

A shrub is usually defined as a woody perennial that branches just above ground level, is reasonably priced and taking into consideration the part that the smaller ones play by acting as ground cover and weed smotherer their rating is very high in the horticultural charts.

Having decided on your own particular soil, decide which shrubs please you most in respect of colour, types of leaf, garden decoration and, for justification of this book, which shrubs will serve you well for cutting in Summer and Autumn.

Moving slowly from late Spring into early Summer, we have such an abundance of flowering shrubs which are suitable for lasting when cut and well conditioned.

All the lilac family (Syringa) in distinct colours of white, yellow, mauve and deep purple and in single and double form, can be arranged to advantage with little or no foliage. This can be done for two reasons; the heads of flowers will last much longer when most of the foliage around these heads is removed. Secondly the end product looks clearer and less cluttered arranged in this way.

At this time the shrub roses are coming into flower and what a joy they are, beautiful arching sprays of single and double flowers; especially lovely flowers for decoration of the garden, and for special occasions indoors. I say for special occasions, because the sprays are covered with open, half open and tightly folded buds, so at all times the scene is changing; some petals dropping, some opening and the buds on the move. I have in mind one of the earliest flowering yellow forms, 'CanaryBird', excellent value for the already mentioned one occasion or wedding decoration.

Moss roses cannot be ignored for their sheer beauty and perfume. This time cut quite short, six to seven inch stems, and used as a central interest in a group of mixed flowers.

Quoting the specialists as I do: There are no other shrubs that have such a long flowering season as the rose. Whereas the shrub roses have a short flowering season, the hybrid teas, the floribundas are blooming on and off the entire summer and when weather conditions are favourable, right up to November and December.

Taking into consideration the use to which the roses and all the other subjects are being put, it is as well to grow flowers for a chosen colour scheme; perhaps white to cream to yellow, or a warm yellow to peach to ochre, and burnt orange to bronze. Grey to soft pink to pale mauve to purple, all these shades and tints can be found in the plant material I have used and mentioned.

Feeding the roses and mulching with farm yard manure is a very pleasant task and rewarding too, when one considers the wealth to be showered on one, months later.

An appropriate time to recall the rewards of manure? I don't know. Several years ago a friend who lived in St. Johns Wood, London, and who had a very lovely formal town garden, was asked by her husband what she would like most for her birthday, to his astonishment came the reply: a load of horse manure.

Constance Spry told a delightful story. To one of her many audiences, she was explaining what great stuff for top dressing roses, was old cow manure. A short silence followed then a voice from the audience enquired how old did the cow have to be!

Believe it or not, as I write, a friend has brought me some plants which I coveted, accompanied by some well rotted cow manure!

Escallonia, Weigela and Kolkwitzia are splendid shrubs to grow in the pale pink to deep rose range, again very lovely arching sprays of bell shaped flowers which can only give grace and movement to any arrangement.

Kerria, with deep yellow flowers, one with double flowers which is the more common, and the other which is infinitely prettier bears elegant sprays of single flowers.

Flowering at the same time, and mentioned p. 55, are the Euphorbias, especially E.wulfenii and E.characias. Lime green flowers on two to five feet stems, hammered and given a drink of deep hot water, they team well with the yellow kerria for arranging.

Mentioned earlier as well was the family of daphnes and here in Hertfordshire, Daphne pontica in May, is in full bloom. Green flowers are borne in abundance, they scent the air very gently all day, while at night the perfume is pumped out to such an extent that from an open window upstairs there is no denying that the lily of the valley type of scent is from this delightful Daphne, see p. 55. The flowers are borne on the tips of the old wood, and as they fade are superseded by the young leaves. It is an evergreen shrub and is therefore a good looking bush all the year round.

For those who like small flowers, the shrubby Spiraeas can be very useful additions to the garden, restrained in growth they form neat bushes with arching sprays festooned with dainty white flowers, or pink or ruby red. Extra special care must be taken when using them for arrangements for the fine woody stems need hammering and given a really deep drink before use.

Hydrangeas in all their delightful colours are invaluable for long lasting garden decoration and as the flower heads mature so they are equally useful for cutting for arrangements in white, pink, pale blue, deep blue and maroon. The stems are sufficiently woody to need splitting and following a deep drink overnight they are then ready for arranging. If for any reason the heads appear drooping and soft to the touch a first aid treatment of wet tissue paper can be applied to each head. If the wilting is not too severe, with the help of the wet paper left on all night, they should have recovered by the morning.

Philadelphus, or mock orange as it is sometimes called, has a short season in flower, but while it lasts it is a glorious shrub for cutting. With many of the larger leaves removed it is an invaluable addition to the garden and can therefore be used for church and home alike. Here in southern England it is in flower during the last two weeks of June. A delightful relative of the former, so useful for the smaller garden, is P.coronarius aureus, which makes compact bushes of yellow-green foliage with the same white orange-blossom like flowers.

I can hear the question being asked 'I wonder why such and such has not been included—flowers like laburnum, wisteria and perhaps several others? The answer must surely be, they simply will not last well in water, so therefore for garden decoration they are superb, but indoors can be very temperamental.

Jasmine, with the star-like white flowers, are excellent for cutting for the perfume alone. Other climbing subjects, like the clematis, of which there are so many from which to choose, give an arrangement that little 'Je ne sais quoi', so important an addition with great character.

Tree peonies leave one absolutely spellbound with their sheer beauty. The flowers, some single, some semi-double and some double, in the most wonderful colour range, from white and cream to pink, deep red to black-red and all furnished with an array of yellow stamens, their beauty does not end here for they have deeply indented foliage in grey green, bearing on the surface of the leaves a bloom reminiscent of grapes. Some of the tree peonies have very fine bronze foliage which can be conditioned and used separately in arrangements.

Climbing honeysuckle and roses in all their varied forms are decorative for the garden and home alike, supported by walls, fences or aged fruit trees perhaps, they can contribute to the long list of suitable subjects for growing in the cottage garden and cutting for arrangements.

Some of the summer flowering brooms can be extremely useful in their own particular colour range of cream, yellow, yellow and red, pink and bronze.

Romneya coulteri, one of the most beautiful members of the poppy family, a sub-shrubby plant with tall herbaceous stems, is a subject of great glamour. On hot, dry, unfed soil it will reach a height of six feet or more, bearing on the tip of the stem and surrounded with buds to make a succession, a single flower of chiffon-like petals of pure white, surrounding a cluster of hundreds of yellow stamens. The grey deeply cut leaves growing alternately the entire length of the stem last well in water for a week or more, likewise the beautiful flowers.

Everyone has their favourite shrub and these mentioned above are some of mine. Many more there are from which to make your own personal choice taking into account the size, aspect, soil and whereabouts of the garden.

2
Growing Herbaceous Plants

The following plants would form an excellent collection for a picking garden, with great variety in colour and form:

Daisy Type Flowers
Anthemis tinctoria
Chrysanthemum maximum varieties
Chrysanthemum singles
Doronicum
Erigeron
Heliopsis
Michaelmas daisies
Pyrethrum
Rudbeckia newmanii
Rudbeckia purpurea
Senecio clivorum

Flowers in Spiked Form:
Aconitum
Astilbes various
Brunnera macrophylla
Delphinium
Dicentra spectabilis
Kniphofias
Lobelia cardinalis
Nepeta 'Six Hills'
Penstemon
Physostegia virginiana
Salvia virgata nemorosa
Sidalcea
Veronica 'Royal Blue'

Round or Pointed heads of Flowers:
Achillea: 'Cerise Queen' and 'Golden Plate'
Alchemilla
Alstroemeria
Anchusa
Anchusa myosotidiflora
Asclepias tuberosa
Bocconia
Heuchera
Phlox
Polyanthus
Thalictrum dipterocarpum

Completely Round Flowers:
Echinops retro
Primula denticulata
Ranunculus
Trollius

Clouds of Minute Flowers:
Gypsophila: pink and white
Saponaria
Statice latifolia

Many flowers worth cultivating as annuals, perennials and biennials fall into none of the foregoing categories, so they can well be listed on their own.

Amaryllis belladonna (late summer flowering bulb)
Anemone hupehensis japonica (late in the year)
Carnations: border
Crinum (late summer flowering bulb)
Dahlias
Gentiana septemfida
Gentiana sino-ornata
Iris
Lychnis arkwrightii
Lychnis chalcedonica
Monarda didyma: scarlet, pink, mauve and white
Nerine (late summer flowering bulb)
Old Fashioned Pinks (for scent and colour)
Oriental poppies: scarlet, pink, shaded and white
Peonies
Scabious

Grey Foliage:
Achillea brachyphylla
Anaphalis triplinervis
Artemesia baumgartenii
Artemesia ludoviciana
Artemesia stelleriana
Centaurea gymnocarpa
Cinereria maritima
Convolvulus cneorum
Romneya coulteri foliage
Rue 'Jackmans' blue
Salvia argentea
Santolina chamaecyparissus
Stachys lanata

Some Yellow and Lime Green Trees, Shrubs and Herbaceous Plants as a Collection:
Bay golden
Box
Catalpa
Coreopsis
Cupressus
Daphne pontica
Elaeagnus pungens maculata
Elder: golden cut-leafed
Golden Rod
Holly
Marigold
Molucella
Nicotiana 'Lime Green'
Philadelphus coronarius aureus
Privet
Verbascum (flower spike)
Yew

Blue and Silver Garden:
Artemesias
Artichoke
Buddleia alternifolia
Buddleia fallowiana
Cardoon
Cerastium
Chamaecyparis lawsoniana 'Triomphe de Boskoop'
Elaeagnus argentea
Eryngium
Euphorbia wulfenii (when mature is grey)
Hosta
Lavender
Nepeta
Onopordon
Pyrus salicifolia pendula
Rue
Santolina
Sea Buckthorn
Senecio greyii
Shepherdia argentea
Yucca

For Edging and Cutting:
Border Pinks
Carnations
Silver Thyme
Verbascum foliage

All flowers are fabulous and some are more fabulous than others. I have in mind of course the lily family, two very easily grown ones are L. candidium and Lilium regale. Either of them cut for decoration give an arrangement a touch of sophistication.

Dahlias have the longest season of flowering, second only to roses, so with care and planning every shade and tint from white through cream, yellow, peach, apricot, to pinks, reds, purples and bronzes are available for growing. To visit a nursery of a dahlia specialist in summer when all the plants are in full bloom is a great experience. Every shade of textile and wall colouring can be matched or complemented, so great is their versatility.

I had the good fortune to be the director of a country wedding during dahlia time, with house, church and marquee to decorate. Carrying the colours of carpets, curtains or a dominant picture in my mind I was able to choose the identical dahlias for the job. With other flowers of course and carefully selected foliage it made a great family day even greater.

Chrysanthemums, an enormous family, the singles, the doubles, the spray, the anemone centred, the rayonanthe are so versatile and well lasting for decorative purposes. Far too numerous to name but with a local grower and a catalogue, a very good selection can be made for growing in the garden and for eventual cutting.

Luck plays an important part with flowers for flower decoration, our unpredictable weather making it impossible to be absolutely sure of some special flower. It is as the Queen said to Alice in *Through the Looking-glass*: 'The rule is, jam tomorrow and jam yesterday—but never jam today.' So with flowers, they were available last week and probably will be next, but never this week. It behoves one to have substitutes firmly tucked away in the back of one's mind.

Flower-arrangement, using flowers and foliage from one's garden, can be tremendously rewarding, moreover, even after a lifetime of planning and arranging for others and oneself, the stimulation and rewards are endless. As one is quite incapable of repeating designs, the word 'boredom' never enters the vocabulary of a true lover of flowers.

3
Flowers and Foliage

Winter and Spring

Throughout the horticultural year in Great Britain there is a wealth of variety, which changes week by week, so at no time are we without some floral treasure.

I remember bemoaning the fact that I and the Almighty together had managed to resuscitate not only a difficult shrub but had managed to get it to bloom. It was out and over in precisely two weeks—which depressed me so much. Instead of being eternally grateful for our joint triumph—I was faced with the depressing thought that I had now to wait a further fifty weeks before this splendid shrub would flower again. I was tersely told that there were plenty of other things to take its place.

Much can, and has been said about large gardens and their contents, but it is the medium sized and small garden with which I am most concerned. In other words where space is restricted the whole matter is reduced to the right priorities, in terms of, how much light a tree or shrub is going to take, how wide a mesh of roots is it going to have—how high and wide will it grow? In fact to be really brutal, the value of its output for its allotted space. How much pleasure it is going to give you as you look at it through the drawing room window in December, January and February, and finally its lasting properties when cut as a bare branch or in leaf, flower or fruit. All these points can be decided in a comfortable armchair, by a good fire and with an authoritative catalogue. Given the correct acid soil, the obvious evergreen shrubs spring to mind: rhododendron, camellia, pieris, azalea and some of the ericas; then come the splendid ones who never ask for anything special, like the eleagnus, variegated and otherwise, laurel, aucuba, the Portugal laurel, griselinia, many daphnes, and of course all the many ivies in their different colourings, the yellow and near white, the grey, the flecked, the smooth and frilly edged—they are all invaluable for cutting in the winter.

December and January are looked upon as very dead and unproductive months by the non gardener, but to the dedicated it is a time of the greatest excitement.

One naturally thinks of Helleborus niger or Christmas rose in the dark days of winter, however there are, with careful selection, hellebores to bloom for ten months of the year. Some are excellent 'lasters' for cutting and the others are best viewed from the other side of the window. Helleborus niger, foetidus and corsicus are splendid for cutting, but abschasicus and orientalis are best admired in the garden, near the house.

There is one consolation for a small garden, everything is near the house. Close for viewing and close for smelling, which brings me once more to the flowering shrubs of mid-winter. Witch-hazel; Hamamelis mollis and winter sweet: Chimonanthus praecox are deliciously scented, so too is Viburnum fragrans (now renamed farreri). Winter jasmine: Jasminum nudiflorum, excellent for cutting and it is blessed with a long flowering season, in fact all three of the dreariest months. Parrotia and Cornus mas and Corylopsis (see colour plate 1) are all excellent and not too large for the small spaces. We continue with catkins; Garrya elliptica makes interesting growing and cutting in midwinter. Very lovely long pale green tassels adorn this evergreen shrub with equal merits for garden house and church. (See p. 56). Hazel catkins, wild and cultivated too, are the first to spring to mind when thinking of this type of inflorescence—in fact all the Salix or willow family are interesting. Pussy-willow can be cut as early as December, the protective brown scales removed, the stems hammered and the silver catkins will expand and grow in water.

Two of the special willows—and there are many from which to choose—are S.daphnoides with beautiful maroon red stems and enormous silver catkins (see p. 49). S. melanostachys an introduction from Japan—with dense black catkins is a little more dramatic; it teams up well with alder cones and catkins which too, are a deep purple/black. The centres of some red tulips are adorned with this same colour, likewise the anthers of their stamens (p. 56).

For stems alone in the willow family there are cream ones, yellow and beige, twisted and fasciated, all equally decorative. To those living near London it is a journey worth while making to visit an early fortnightly show of the Royal Horticultural Society where one can see so many of these really lovely shrubs.

There too it is worth studying the dogwood family so decorative in the winter garden with its many coloured stems of varying shades of reds and yellows. Growing very straight as they do, but with gentle massage they can be coaxed into a curve for arrangement (see colour plate 1). Returning for one moment to the twisted willow and similarly twisted hazel. It was that great horticulturalist and crocus expert Mr. E. A. Bowles who explained to me how this unusual characteristic comes about. This natural hybrid, the Hazel, which in fact Mr. Bowles discovered in a hedgerow has a fast growing wood with a slow growing bark so it can be seen quite easily that as the wood grows away, so the bark holds it back and causes the characteristic contortions—described in its Latin name contorta.

Prunus subhirtella 'autumnalis' and 'rosea' are a great joy to behold in full flower on leafless stems in December. Our temperature fluctuating as it does throughout the winter in Great Britain gives us so many horticultural surprises—the prunus may be in full flower for two or three weeks, when a cold snap will hold it back—a warm patch arrives and suddenly it will burst into flower again, revealing the soft pink petals of these star like flowers.

Great battles flourish at local flower shows between those who say that Euphorbia wulfenii and Euphorbia characias are not shrubs and those who say they are—well it is not for me to say, but you will find them listed amongst the shrubs of the leading nurseries and the hardy herbaceous perennials. The glaucus foliage throughout the winter and the lime green flowers all the summer supply you with something that architecturally is very interesting and a colour that is not easily found in any other subject.

As we pass, almost without noticing, into official Spring, we are overwhelmed with prunus, malus, in all their colours, so prolific are they that it is difficult to pick out any special one, except perhaps Prunus Tai Haku, the double white, where the centre of each double flower is tinged with green. The permanent shrubs and trees are just the right setting for underplanting of narcissi, tulips and further in the year, lilies and other bulbous subjects.

Amongst the long list of shrubs which are recommended for winter colour and interest in the small garden and available for cutting, I would put the evergreen and variegated elaeagnus E.ebbingii with silvery green foliage, white scented flowers in October, November and December. E.pungens aurea variegata with green and bright yellow centred leaves throughout the year.

Daphnes—well known for their fragrance—are a delight in the garden, and for cutting for small bouquets in the country church. With stems split and an initial drink of hot water, they can be persuaded to last for several days.

D. laureola, indigenous to this country, with green flowers from December to April.

D. mezereum, deep purplish pink flowers February–March.

D. pontica, lime green flowers in bloom spasmodically January–May.

D. odora marginata variegata, lanceolate green leaves edged with cream/yellow, with sweetly scented deep pink flowers in February–March.

The Mahonia family or Oregon Grape by virtue of their being evergreen are so useful for winter decoration. M. aquifolium— lustrous green leaves which turn bronze/purple in the autumn.

M. bealei—a very large leafed berberis with spikes of yellow lily-of the-valley scented flowers.

There are many, many more Mahonias, some evergreen and some deciduous—and everyone well worth growing.

Quince or Chaenomeles, a flowering shrub of distinction, with either pale pink flowers, deep pink, salmon pink and pink ochre. They last well in water.

Abeliophyllum is a shrub worthy of special mention, small white forsythia-like flowers with orange centres and a sweet scent, opening in February–March.

Atriplex halimus is a must for the winter garden, a small sized shrub of medium height, with grey/green leaves. The arching sprays last extremely well in water.

Corylopsis—grown in a sheltered border—one is rewarded with long drooping spikes of scented primrose yellow flowers which last well when cut for home or church.

Eucalyptus grown where it can have some shelter is a very useful blue/grey foliage for cutting. It lasts for weeks in water.

Hamamelis. The Witchhazels—do not like lime. They thrive in a well drained soil where peat or leafmould has been added. One is finally rewarded with large flowers of many sulphur yellow twisted petals, frost immune and sweetly scented which last for weeks.

Magnolia. Several members in cultivation are in flower, and long lasting in water, as early as March. One small growing is M. stellata and a little larger one M. soulangeana (see colour plate 3).

Parrotia. Excellent shrub for cutting during its flowering period of January–March. Small tufted red flowers not unlike the Witch Hazel we know, to which it is closely related.

Prunus. The almonds, peaches, plums, sloes and cherries, many of which bloom in early spring are: P. communis, Common almond. P. davidiana alba a flowering peach for February. P. pissardii nigra with pale pink flowers in March and deep rich purple leaves as the year progresses.

The cherries I have already mentioned. P. subhirtella autumnalis is the most important for months of spasmodic flowering throughout the winter. It will last for several days in water.

The Ivy family makes a great contribution to flower arrangement, medium and large arrangements alike, one cannot fault them. From the gardeners point of view they are all hardy, all evergreen, easy to propagate and very difficult to kill. They last well in water and by their very nature of different shape, size and variegation—are invaluable as a foil to flower arrangement.

Hedera canariensis.

Hedera canariensis variegata.

Hedera dentata variegata—palest grey-green and creamy white.

Hedera caenwoodiana—long-fingered pointed leaves of dark green.
Hedera marginata major—beautiful mixtures of milk-white, grey-green and grey occur in varying proportions on every leaf.
Hedera 'Silver Queen'—variegated in cream and green, often pink-edged.
Hedera helix cristata—the green frilly edged ivy, bears the usual trail but light green in its youth.

As there is a great revival of the ivy as a house plant and perhaps more so as a garden plant, I have therefore only listed the more usual ones, but for the dedicated I recommend a visit to the Royal Horticultural Society's fortnightly shows, or better still the nearest Garden Centre where one can not only see and admire but buy container grown plants to take home. We all enjoy the spontaneity of buying some treasure on the spot, bearing it home in triumph for immediate planting.

Camellia—the acid soil loving shrub—with the Rhododendron and Azalea, their numbers are legion. One is able to cut branches for decoration from large specimens. There are some hybrids which are fast growing and bloom from February to May.

Camellia 'Donation'—a large semi-double clear pink flower.

Inspiration—a paler pink to 'Donation'.

J.C. Williams—a large single pale pink with an exciting array of yellow stamens in the centre.

There are few rhododendrons and azaleas for winter flowering, but if it is a must for you then visit your nearest specialist nursery, when the advice of local conditions and aspect will be freely given. A comprehensive catalogue will help with the enormous choice.

Herbaceous plants are our next concern, interesting and useful foliage and flowers with good long lasting qualities for cutting and using indoors during winter and spring.

Bergenia comes first to my mind. Good solid leaves, five, six and seven inches across—a good deep green. They will last in water for two or three weeks (see colour plate 1).

Arum italicum—an invaluable plant. Like our own wild arum growing in the hedgerows—this Italian arum is even more useful for it comes into leaf in the Autumn. The shape of an arrowhead, it bears the most beautiful marble like markings, white on the shining dark green leaves (see pp. 51, 53, 55).

It likes the same conditions as its English cousin, a damp position with not too much sun, in fact dappled sunlight as one catalogue so poetically describes it. Although preoccupied with winter and spring, I must mention here, the extra bonus of the A. italicum given to us in June–July. The flower is typical of all arums and seven or eight inches long, but the colour is like nothing else, the most beautiful, ethereal soft light green, as year after year, I never cease to wonder at its sheer beauty.

A splendid evergreen iris which must not be forgotten I. foetidissima dark green shining leaves all the year round and its variegated counterpart—I. foetidissima variegata. They both have insignificant grey flowers in summer, but beautiful sprays of orange berries in autumn.

Assuming that we have the space to spare, a cutting border of daffodils, narcissi, tulips and hyacinths is an economy and a delight. By studying an illustrated catalogue of the bulb specialist it is possible to have a selection of early spring flowers for cutting.

There are many daffodils to choose from, different colours, shapes, sizes, height and time of flowering—likewise narcissi. They are all listed with great simplicity for ease of choice of the customer in the comprehensive catalogue. 'February Gold' one of the earliest of the narcissi—deep yellow with fly-away petals which form the perianth, is a deliciously scented flower and long lasting, when used for cutting.

'Irene Copeland' is a beautiful creamy-white double flowered narcissus.

'Spellbinder' is a tall growing daffodil of great substance—as my catalogue describes it, and then it goes on to say: 'A large and quite distinct clear luminous greeny sulphur-lemon, when fully developed, the inside of the flanged trumpet passes almost to white, while the outside of the trumpet retains its colour and the serrated brim is tipped with sparkling lemon.' Certainly a description worth quoting, word for word.

Another great favourite of mine is 'Mount Hood', a good strong daffodil, cream as it first comes out and shades to white, with strong stems of up to eighteen inches in length.

There are so many narcissi to choose from that perhaps it is more satisfactory to do so with the growers beautifully illustrated catalogue or, if one is able, to visit a grower in the Spring to enjoy the breathtaking experience.

There are so many beautiful bulbous subjects available for growing in one's own garden it is difficult to know which ones to leave out. It is the larger ones for medium sized arrangements with which we are now concerned—narcissi and daffodils, and now tulips and hyacinths.

Tulips are legion—so it is important to consult a specialist book, or a well illustrated catalogue. In the narrowest sense, if only growing for your own home decoration, it is as well to consider the predominant colourings of the entrance hall and living rooms, then revolving around these colourings it makes the choice of bulb much easier. However, as we are considering flowers for use outside the home as well—for church decoration and local shows—then a wider choice is necessary; with a cutting border you can have a really good selection made up of a few bulbs of your particular choice of colours normally associated with the church calendar. Remember tulips can be in flower in the open ground from March to the end of May. So one not only has the months of blooming, and the colour, but the height to which they will grow and the shape to consider.

Tulip Species are the first to bloom, then come the:
Early Single Tulips
Early Double Tulips
Mid-Season Tulips made up of Mendel and Triumph Tulips
Darwin Tulips and The Darwin Hybrids come next, tall and stately in a brilliant range of colours.
Lily-flowered tulips for May flowering come next on the list, tall and stately with strong stems, they support a longish shaped head of beautiful reflexing petals.

Cottage tulips are next and are May flowering, and at the same time come Peony-flowered tulips, very striking double flowers in very varied colours.

Parrot Tulips should not be left out of this collection. Picturesque in the garden and they are fine for cutting. They have been in our gardens since the year 1665.

Fringed Tulips must not be forgotten, they are so beautiful and so unusual.

Viridiflora Tulips are a great asset for decoration. As their name suggests they are all shaded with green.

Kaufmanniana and Greigii and Fosteriana Tulips must be mentioned here, though for our purpose of medium sized arrangements they are very much shorter in the stem and therefore useful for the colour.

Hyacinths, cut for decoration add the extra fragrance and the weight that is important to the balance of any arrangement, be it flowers with complimentary foliage, or foliage alone.

'Prepared' hyacinths for early forcing are of course for indoor culture—where the 'Unprepared' can be grown out-of-doors for garden decoration, likewise picking.

For a medium sized flower arrangement three stems of hyacinths should be sufficient to bring the weight towards the centre of the group, emphasising the focal point, or the centre of the design.

Hyacinths can be obtained in the following colours:

White	Porcelain Blue
Pale pink	Dark Blue
Pink	Yellow
Red	

Summer and Autumn

Quite impossible as it is to define the two seasons we can now consider all the trees, shrubs, perennial and annual flowers for the summer and autumn garden, which will provide material for cutting for medium and large sized arrangements.

I need hardly say that great care is needed when choosing trees for the smaller garden. Take a trip to the local nurseryman and garden centre, having first browsed through the specialist catalogue and horticultural encyclopaedia to check on maximum heights, types of soil required for your choice of plant. The lime lovers and haters have to have very careful treatment, likewise the peat lovers. consider too, trees which flower in the late spring and early summer, have beautiful young foliage and by the time Autumn comes around they are changing to all the breathtaking colours of that time of the year.

Amongst the many acers; the maples and the sycamores there are a few varieties which form small to medium trees. A. palmatum and A. henryi are two examples of this. When cut for church and home the foliage must be mature and very careful attention must be given to the conditioning; hammered stems and a deep drink overnight must be given to ensure good lasting.

Several acers are listed as small specimen trees, Betula pendula, a charming birch and several cotoneasters, such as: C. salicifolius 'Autumn Fire', C. rotundifolius, C. simonsii and C. wardii.

Many varieties of magnolia can be classed here, especially M. stellata.

Prunus, incorporating peaches, plums and cherries growing in small sizes and cut with the greatest care for indoor decoration are invaluable for the small garden, so too are the ornamental Crab Apples or Malus. Robinia, coming into leaf in middle spring has beautiful pinnate leaves of brilliant lime green. Though branches are not good lasting from this tree, single leaves well conditioned will last extremely well in arrangements.

Pyrus salicifolia 'pendula', the Willow leaf pear, is delightful to grow and useful for cutting.

Many of the 'Mountain Ash' family, the Sorbus, are easily contained in the small garden, their berries turning to white, yellow, pink, red and orange, according to the variety, with autumn coloured foliage second to none.

A particularly rewarding sorbus is whitebeam or Sorbus aria, excellent for planting as a specimen tree, and now very effectively used by the more imaginative urban boroughs for avenue planting. Very good lasting in water, giving grey downy foliage on both sides of the leaf in spring and gradually changing to green on the upper surface and grey beneath as the seasons change.

One cannot end a chapter on horticulture by saying: 'Now lastly' for there is just no end to the species and cultivars available for growing and for cutting. Where space is limited one can only choose some favourites which will fulfil the dual purpose.

4
Preserving and Drying Materials

Very gradually as the last months of the year come into sight, the garden and hedgerow scene changes from the summer greens to the reds, browns and orange of berries, the breathtaking colours of the leaves to the final dropping of all the leaves of deciduous trees. While our trees remain in exciting shape, colour and form as skeletons throughout the winter, we can then keep our preserved material to remind us of the earlier part of the year.

Dried subjects used for church should, I think, be used with restraint. They are generally speaking more pleasing when employed as a setting for the last few flowers of the year. Perhaps using the last clear coloured and heavily scented roses from the garden or five really lovely chrysanthemums.

Like everything else in life, one has to learn when to stop. Over filling of a container is something one has to become aware of by practice. To enjoy the structure of seed heads and branches, restraint is the keyword, likewise the length of time the arrangement is on display is best limited. Many of us have become prejudiced against dried arrangements for either the flowers are not used with allied colours, or the dried material has been dyed in the most stunning, and unnatural colours. Perhaps most important of all, as dust intervenes to dim the textures which were once pleasing, and no amount of blowing restores them to their former beauty, then is the time to be very firm with oneself and with a purposeful gait, make smartly for the bonfire.

Time for cutting

The best time for harvesting your cultivated or wild material for preserving and drying must largely be dictated by the weather conditions. In Great Britain one can experience (as Bob Hope once said) all four seasons in one day. However to be realistic one should watch the required leaves and flowers daily, cut the stems about midday in order that any dew that has fallen overnight has completely dried off.

Taking wild cow parsley, or wild chervil, or wild parsnip as an example, with weather conditions right, sunny with a breeze is the best time, the flowers should all be over, seed set, with the stem beginning to dry off, cut them carefully and as they tangle so easily, loosely wrap two or three stems together in newspaper and tie the stems and paper firmly ready for drying. On arrival at the allotted spot, the shed, garage or spare bedroom, hang up the separate parcels and very gently tear away half the newspaper to facilitate the circulation of air.

Methods of preserving

The rewards of leaving a good selection of seed heads on plants from the ensuing seasons is inestimable.

Many seed heads can be tied up in bunches and dried in an airy shed, while flowers can be preserved in various ways, chemically and otherwise, or pressed to make flower pictures. Leaves of garden and forest trees can all be treated to give so much pleasure as arrangements for the coming winter.

Branches of shrubs berried or merely in leaf keep very well indeed. Single leaves such as aspidistra or raspberry, or garden fern, or giant fern Osmunda regalis and our wild bracken all require different treatment of preservation but the final results are worth all the trouble and patience that has gone into the work.

Some flowering annuals and perennials can be preserved in the most breath-taking way, so well done are they that the petals are erect and the colours exactly the same as when they were cut from the plant. Just as pleasing are the flowers that have been dried in a different way, but have faded very slightly. These muted shades are just as lovely and very soothing to the eye and one is reminded of the term, faded elegance—a true description of fading furniture that has caught the sun, of tapestries placed in the sunlight, or brushed with cold tea in order to reach the soft liveable colours that are so attractive. The faded edges of velvet curtains so soft and muted as though done deliberately, these are shades and tints of flowers and foliage dried by standing upright in a vessel, or those hung upside down in a warm airy place.

A plantsman or the real lover of plants knows the shape of the seed he is sowing, how it will look on germination, in its youth and what he hopes it will look like in maturity, in leaf, flower and fruit. Its special peculiarities, such as unusual bracts or stipules to the leaf, all these points add to the interest of growing, drying and finally arranging one's own harvest.

Methods of drying:

Hanging
Upright drying
Drying in water
Drying flat
Drying flat with dessicants
Drying and pressing
Ironing
Preserving in glycerine and water

Materials for Hanging:

ACANTHUS, BEARS' BREECHES. Hardy Perennial. Flower and Seed Heads.

ACHILLEA, YARROW. Hardy Perennial. Can be dried hanging or standing upright. (The fact which determines whether stems should be upright or hanging, is whether the stem is sufficiently strong to support the weight of the head).

ACROCLINIUM (now known as HELIPTERUM) Half hardy annual. Very pretty semi-double everlasting flower in pink and more unusually in white and yellow.

ALLIUM: CHIVES, ONION, GARLIC INCLUDING SPECIES AND CULTIVARS now grown for decoration dry well, hung in bunches.

ALDER, COMMON ALDER (ALNUS GLUTINOSAS)

ANAPHALIS TRIPLINERVIS or GNAPHALIUM or IMMORTELLS Perennial one to two feet, wooly grey leaves with clusters of small double white everlasting papery flowers.

BELLS OF IRELAND (MOLUCELLA LAEVIS) Half Hardy Annual.

BOCCONIA: PLUME POPPY. Perennial. Flower spikes dry well.

BULRUSH, COMMON ENGLISH NAME. Perennial. CAT TAIL. A stately subject. Care must be taken not to damage the head as it can burst or shatter, when everything and everybody is covered in dandelion-like down. when completely dried off a good preventative against shattering is a shot or two of hair lacquer all over the head of the Bulrush.

CAPE GOOSEBERRY (PHYSALIS FRANCHETTI GIGANTEA and PYGMEA. Perennial. A beautiful fresh warm orange lantern. As a child I used to slit some lanterns into five segments with a razor blade, bend them carefully back exposing the central orange berry, wiring each one on to a beech twig. Very striking with added preserved fern in a copper container.

CLARKIA. Hardy Annual. Pink, White and Pink and Purple. Can be preserved very well if dried quickly.

CLEMATIS. Perennial. CULTIVATED SPECIES and CULTIVARS.

WILD SPECIES (OLD MAN'S BEARD or VITALBA, TRAVELLERS JOY).

CLEMATIS TANGUTICA. The long stems of fluffy seed heads are best dried off then sprayed with hair lacquer.

DELPHINIUM Perennial. CANDLE LARKSPUR. When the lowest flowers on a spike are mature, the secondary flowers are about to open and the buds at the top are still green, this is the time to hang and dry quickly in a heated room perhaps.

DIANTHUS—PINKS, COTTAGE PINKS. Their fawn coloured seed heads are very useful for small arrangements.

DOCK, Biennial (SHEEP SORREL). Lovely rust red seed heads can either be hung to dry or preserved in glycerine and water.

FOXGLOVE. Mostly Biennial—DIGITALIS. Arching side shoots as well as the main stem dry very well.

'GLOBE' ARTICHOKE (CYNARA CARDUNCULUS) Biennial and Perennial.

GLOBE THISTLE. Perennial. (ECHINOPS RITRO). Grey leaves and inflorescences lavendar blue-grey dry out in the most spectacular way.

GODETIA. Annual. Dried quickly the double flowers of white and white suffused pink are a useful addition to the collection of middle height subjects.

GOLDEN ROD. Perennial. SOLIDAGO RIGIDA. Parched soil seems to be a good spot to grow golden rod. Dried it is just a shade more mellow than when growing, a soft warm yellow, shading to beige and later a light brown.

GRASSES. Annual and Perennial. One of our leading seed merchants lists no less than forty-one different grasses, ranging from the smallest to the tallest, which includes ZEA or SWEET CORN or MAIZE—all of them will dry well, but select them carefully and try out the stem test, if they are weak when maturing it may be better to dry them flat on a tray or box lid.

HEATHERS ERICA great lovers of peat and sandy soil. When the flowers are opening at the bottom of the spike, this is the time to dry them off, upside down or with hammered stems in water.

HELICHRYSUM. STRAW FLOWER or STRAW DAISY. Mixed Soil.
EVERLASTING so says the seed catalogue and then continues twelve variations of the main theme—so you take your choice. Good for growing in a cutting border in full sun. A few very strong stems stripped of their leaves will dry well hanging, but a better way is to cut the mature flowers into a box lid and immediately insert into the half inch hollow stem a wire about seven inches long and of a 22 gauge. This must not show in the face of the flower, if it does pull it back a fraction so no dark point of the wire is visible. It is found that as the stem is moist the wire rusts and so fixes the flower very firmly. There is therefore no need to bind the stem, merely when dry to cover the one to two inch stem with gutta-percha and bend into realistic shapes.

HOGWEED—COW PARSNIP. A NATIVE OF THE HEDGEROW.

HONESTY LUNARIA. Hardy Biennial. when the two outer covers of the seed pods are removed, the centre silver layer remains—so useful for the cream to white range, the high-key colouring.

HOP. HUMULUS LUPULUS. COMMON HOP. A Hardy Annual. Their long trailing stems bearing the flowers of the Hop can be dried hanging up or preserved in glycerine and water.

HORSE TAIL SPIKES. EQUISETUM. A plant growing wild. The cone like inflorescences dry well on their six to twelve inch stems either hanging, or perhaps better still supported in a jam jar.

IRIS. Any seed heads inadvertently left on the plants make splendid stately stems for decoration.

LARKSPUR. An annual in deep rose, pink, deep purple, pale grey mauve and white. Dried at the same state of development as the delphinium, they are a great asset to the collection.

LAVENDER. Hardy Annual. LAVANDULA need hardly be mentioned as we must all have seen our Mothers tying up little bundles in the late summer for placing between the piles of sheets in the linen cupboard.

LOVE-IN-A-MIST. Hardy Annual. NIGELLA. One can hardly resist cutting the delicate blue flowers, or the globular seed heads surrounded by green whiskers.

LUPIN. Hardy Perennial. LUPINS. Grey furry seed pods like a lot of the pea and bean family, dry well for decoration.

PAMPAS GRASS. Hardy Perennial. CORTADERIA. A stately grass, excellent for very large arrangements.

PEONY VARIOUS. TREE. HERBACEOUS. Lovely seed heads for drying.

PLANTAIN LILY. Perennial. HOSTA. Fading flower spikes give a light pointed shape to an arrangement.

POPPY. Annual. Perennial. PAPAVER. So many delightful seed heads to choose from in this vast group.

PRIMROSE, EVENING. Biennial OENOTHERA. Fine spikes for drying.

RUDBECKIA. Half Hardy Annual. CONEFLOWER and Perennials. Remove the petals leaving the brown black centre to dry on long stems.

SEA HOLLY. Hardy Perennial. ERYNGIUM. Very striking steel blue and grey foliage and flowers. Many varieties to choose from and all very prickly. They are happy in ordinary friable soil.

SHOO-FLY PLANT. Annual. NICANDRA. Attractive fruits dry well on the main stem, after removing foliage.

SYCAMORE, MAPLE and other ACERS—HORNBEAM and ASH—All five trees have the most beautiful winged seeds, they can be cut, defoliated and hung up to dry, or as soon as they are mature they can be placed in a solution of glycerine and water and there left for perhaps three weeks, taken out and dried off.

TEASEL. Hardy Biennial. DIPSACUS SILVESTRIS. COMMON TEASEL. One cannot go wrong with these, they dry so easily, but beware of the very prickly stems.

THISTLE. Hardy Perennial. ONOPORDON or COTTON THISTLE. Wicked spines, but most rewarding is this giant thistle when dried.

XERANTHEMUM. Half Hardy Annual. Very pretty ever-lasting flowers.

Materials for Upright drying

Our second way of drying various subjects is to stand them in good heavy vessels and leave them until they feel brittle to the touch. With only a little experience of this subject one very quickly becomes aware of whether 'a', should be hanging and 'b' standing upright and in a matter of three to four weeks all is ready for arranging.

Some of the heavier stemmed material already mentioned will dry just as well standing upright, for example:

ACANTHUS
ACHILLEA
AGAPANTHUS SEED HEADS
ALLIUM (some of the stronger stemmed ones)
ALDER
ATRIPLEX
BOCCONIA
BULRUSH
GLOBE ARTICHOKE
GLOBE THISTLE
GOLDEN ROD
SWEET CORN
HONESTY
HOGWEED
IRIS
PAMPAS GRASS
SEA HOLLY
SYCAMORE SEEDS
HORNBEAM SEEDS
LICHEN BRANCHES (from the West Country and Scotland)

Materials for Drying in water

This is the third way of drying. This particular method can be applied to the mature heads of hydrangea. By about August, September in Great Britain the flower heads of Hydrangea, whether they have been pink, maroon, blue or white, begin to change colour taking on a greenish tinge, the bracts of each floret become thicker to the touch, this is the time to cut the stems for drying. Remove all the leaves as they do not last in water. Split the stems to allow the water to be taken up, place hydrangea into warm water in a warm room. They will be ready for use in about ten days, perfectly preserved, good muted colours of the original with no shrivelling of the 'petals' (see pp. 70–71 and colour plate 16).

The people who have not had success with hydrangea have cut the heads before they are mature, this has been proved conclusively, so one has to be patient.

Materials for Drying Flat

Many of the more fragile grasses already mentioned for hanging will dry flat on sheets of paper on a shelf in a warm room, while gourds dry out best in the sun or airing cupboard for four weeks or more.

Drying flat with dessicants

There are three substances for the drying of flowers. One is sand, then there is household Borax and silica gel crystals crushed to a powder.

Whichever one chooses to use the method is the same. Cover the base of an airtight polythene box with the dessicant very gently supporting the petals of the flower in one hand shake on the powder and lay it on the layer already in the box. When all the flowers are placed separately in the box with nothing touching anything else, the final layer of dessicant is shaken on gently. The lid replaced and put in a safe place to dry out. When removing the flowers from the box shake off all superfluous dessicant.

Roses, sweet peas, violets, carnations and many of like texture take from two to five days to dry out.

On several occasions I have been asked to dismantle the bride's bouquet and treat it in the manner already described. One particular bouquet of cymbidiums and lily-of-the-valley at a wedding in Ghent, Belgium, was duly taken to pieces for drying on the night of the wedding, this then had to be remade to the shape of the original bouquet, but slightly shallower, in order that the framer could fix it in a deep frame, with glass and there it remains to this day. A beautiful reminder of the bride's wedding day, a fashionable trend in Belgium during this last decade.

Materials for Drying and Pressing

When a very small child I remember my Mother pressing between two sheets of newspaper, branches of russet red beech and the green fern DRYOPTERIS FILIX-MAS which in a sheltered place remains throughout the winter. These two and bracken from the woods were carefully placed under the carpet to dry and press, when taken out after two or three weeks they made a very striking arrangement. Individual raspberry leaves pressed, dried and ironed and finally mounted up on twigs provide a soft grey green colour in an arrangement.

OSMUNDA REGALIS, the royal fern, which likes to grow with its feet in mud, at the side of a lake, dries well under pressure and when taken out ironing with a warm iron just finishes the treatment.

IRIS leaves, the sword like leaves of MONTBRETIA and the corrugated leaves of CROCOSMIA (Montbretia's near relative) benefit very much from a warm iron.

Materials for Preserving with Glycerine and Water

One could almost say that this is a foolproof exercise, as there are so few principles to apply. There are now two methods of preserving living material in this way, by firstly dissolving commercial glycerine (one part glycerine to two parts water) with very hot water stirring or shaking until it is all dissolved or equally dispersed solution, or using motor vehicle anti-freeze with an equal quantity of hot water.

Having selected the branches, seed heads and berries, or individual leaves for this particular method of preserving, timing it exactly right, according to the maturity and the weather, then is the time to begin the operation.

For most forest and wayside trees they must be cut during mid-summer when the leaves are not too young but mature, the ends of the stems split for about two inches to allow for uninterrupted drinking. The narrower the vessel holding the solution the better, as it is so much more economical. Every few days check the level of the solution, if it has dropped considerably top it up with hot water so that it is three or four inches deep throughout the time. Keep an eye on the foliage, taking beech as the most common example, when this has turned to a golden brown in either one, two or three weeks, take it out, dry off the stems, it is now ready for use.

Points to look for when preserving in this way. If the tips of the branches are brittle to the touch then the solution has not been taken up satisfactorily, perhaps not sufficiently split at the end of the stem. Now at the other end of the scale, if one sees small beads of moisture on the surface of the leaves it has been left in the solution too long. The branches are taking up more of the solution than they can absorb, so the cycle must be stopped immediately, the stems taken out, dried off and every leaf wiped of excess moisture. A soul destroying job. It is better therefore to be vigilant for several days than to have to add an unnecessary chore to the daily round.

It would be impossible to list all the possibilities for preserving in this way, but here follows a good cross section:

ASPIDISTRA—SINGLE LEAVES
BAY
BELLS OF IRELAND: MOLUCELLA
BERBERIS
BLACKBERRY—when leaves and berries are taken out of the solution spray the berries with hair lacquer
BROOM
ELAEAGNUS: WOOD OLIVE—VARIEGATED and PLAIN
EUCALYPTUS
FATSIA JAPONICA
FOREST and OTHER TREES and SHRUBS (ACERS, MAPLES, BEECH) BRANCHES: GREEN and COPPER
GARRYA ELLIPTICA: TASSEL BUSH
GRISELINIA
HOLLY and BERRIES—after treatment spray berries with lacquer
LIME BRANCHES—in this case remove the leaves and retain only the bracts with flowers or seeds
OAK
PEONY: PAEONIA—Tree peony leaves are the most handsome
RHODODENDRON
ROSE HIPS
ROSEMARY
SHOO FLY PLANT: NICANDRA—Treat in solution then hang up to dry
SILVER BIRCH BRANCHES
SNOWBERRY: SYMPHORICARPUS
SORBUS
SYCAMORE: ACER
VIBURNUM—TRY ALL EVERGREEN ONES

Once the preserved material has been dried off it can be stored away for the future or used as a framework for flower arrangements throughout the winter, or used on its own as an arrangement of subtle colouring, and most interesting textures.

5
Day-by-Day Seasonal Arrangements

Something living in a place of worship adds interest and warmth to the building, just as much as it does in one's own home.

The flower arrangements shown in this chapter portray the possibilities for church decoration throughout the year, in between the days of church festivals and Sunday services, in fact flowers for every day.

Immediately after Christmas and its octave, the buildings look extremely bare, denuded of the foliage and flowers which make Christmas such a lovely festival—then is the time to plant up a trough of indoor plants, of varying heights and interest. Some need good daylight but not direct sunlight so they are eminently suited to a north facing window sill, or a shady porch. The alternative could be a welcoming dish of plants and early flowering hyacinths (see p. 46)— placed near the main entrance of a small church, at table height, so that it can be viewed below eye level.

With careful drainage and watering the planted garden can be made to last a month or more. Hyacinths which will be shorter lived can be removed as their flowers fade and longer lasting plants can take their place. The whole garden will benefit from a light spray of water once or twice a week, which of course will keep the moss looking green and healthy. The more permanent indoor plants with the smooth strong leaves need to have the surface of the leaves carefully washed over regularly as the ever present fine dust in the air inhibits their growth.

These day-by-day arrangements show how an interesting and good lasting addition to church decoration can be made, almost entirely from garden flowers and foliage.

*   *   *

Many of our like-minded Christians of Norway, Finland, Italy, Portugal and Israel feel as we do. Some indoor plants fill the need for something growing, and small as they are, potted begonias in full flower grace many of their altars.

Winter into Spring

House Plants for Winter Decoration

Container: Serving dish. (Transfer printed Willow Pattern 1820–30)

Contents: Begonia rex
Carex japonica, grass
Cyclamen, white, scented with marbled leaves
Fatshedera lizei variegata
Helxine
Hyacinth
Nephrolepis todioides
Peperomia magnoliaefolia variegata
Selaginella

Description: January and February are difficult months for flower decoration. The scarcity of material is one problem and central heating the other. A group of indoor plants arranged as illustrated is the perfect answer. These two planted gardens with undersoil drainage, displayed in lovely old serving dishes are easy to maintain and give tremendous pleasure over a period of many weeks. The popularity of foliage plants has become widespread and their subtle colours, textures and shapes show to advantage against the less cluttered backcloth of the fabric of the church.

The gardens are finished off with green moss, lichen bark, lumps of limestone rock and granite chips, a diversity of textures adding to the already interesting ones of the plants.

Stage 1

Stage 2

Stage 3

47

Winter Flowering Trees and Shrubs

Container: Italian pottery shell, supported by dolphins.
Contents: Alnus glutinosa: Alder
Berberis aquifolia
Bergenia cordifolia
Berried ivy
Cornus alba: Dogwood
Hamamelis mollis: Witch hazel
Parrotia persica
Tulip 'Orange Triumph'

Description: Branches of winter flowering trees and shrubs are used as a foil to flame tulips. In a contemporary container of Italian pottery, this sparse arrangement forms an interesting silhouette against a plain background (see colour plate 1).

The alder in mid-winter and early spring bears reddish catkins on the new wood and the previous year's cones on the older wood. The two together give a wonderful appearance in silhouette against a clear sky when growing on the tree. It naturally follows that an arrangement of shapely stems and interesting lines such as the ones I have arranged here should show to advantage against a plain wall, or clear glass window.

In the same colour range comes the red stem of the cornus, the berberis leaves and the bergenia. The parrotia, rather less common, consists of a cluster of numerous stamens, which have reddish anthers, and the bracts, from which the flowers spring, are a rich brown. The two together appear on the leafless stems, giving a reddish hazy effect in sunshine.

The purplish red calyx of the hamamelis flowers can be seen to the right of the picture.

Flame tulips with a black centre, called 'Orange Triumph', combine in colour to make this collection of flowers, branches and foliage ranging from flame to bronze.

A Group for Winter against the light

Arranged in a large shallow pottery dish (see opposite page) with rocks and moss are:
Arum italicum, leaves
Balsam poplar (Green catkins)
Helleborus corsicus
Ivy and Snowdrops
Pussy willow (Salix daphnoides)

Window sill arrangement

Container: Shallow pottery dish
  Contents: Iris stylosa (unguicularis)
              Winter sweet: Chimonanthus praecox
Description: Suitable for clear glass background, in January and February. Well chosen branches—when cutting— give the group the voids so necessary when displaying arrangements against the light. A pin-holder supports the iris.

An Arrangement of Garden Flowers in a Basket

Contents: Arum italicum, green marbled leaves
         Hyacinths, white
         Kerria japonica, Single yellow buttercup-like flowers
         Lamium, yellow dead-nettle
         Malus, Crab apple
         Narcissus, 'Cheerfulness'
         Polyanthus, yellow and pink

Description: Crab apple and kerria branches form the shape of this basket of spring flowers. Tightly closed buds, with half and fully opened narcissi.

In shades of white, cream, yellow and pink colouring they tone well with the wicker basket.

A Japanese Bronze Vase

Container: Japanese bronze vase 19 in./50 cm. Decorated in relief with birds on flowering prunus branches.

Contents: Cardoon leaves

Wild plum or blackthorn or sloe or prunus spinosa

Description: The branches of blackthorn picked in early spring from the hedgerow, reflect the classic shapes of those shown in the design on the vase. Useful for table or floor.

Cherry, Tulips and Crown Imperials

Container: Tazza in off-white pottery
Contents: Arum italicum
            Cardoon: Cynara cardunculus
            Crown Imperial: Fritillaria imperialis
            Daphne pontica
            Hosta crispula
            Narcissi, poeticus
            Tulips, 'White Triumphator' 'Golden Harvest'
            Viburnum burkwoodii
            Wild cherry

Description: The silhouette of beautiful shapes displayed against a light background. White, cream and clear pale yellow are the colours in this large and informal group.

An Informal Group in a Stoneware Jug. A Collection from the Open Garden

Description: A symphony of mixed greens, arranged high on the handle side of the jug and sweeping away to the lip on the far side. Equally suited to church table or perhaps chancel steps.

(See opposite for contents).

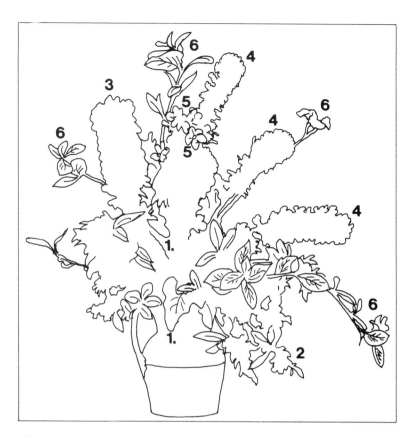

Contents: Arum italicum. (*1*)
Daphne pontica. (*2*)
Euphorbia characias, spurge. (*3*)
Euphorbia wulfenii, spurge. (*4*)
Helleborus corsicus.(*5*)
Sorbus aria, white beam. (*6*)

Tulips, Narcissi and Garrya Elliptica
(Late winter/early spring)
Container: Dessert dish of hammered pewter
Contents: Arum italicum
            Bergenia cordifolia
            Echeveria
            Garrya elliptica
            Helleborus orientalis
            Ivy
            Narcissi, 'Carlton', 'Fortune'
            Tulips, 'Kaiser Kroon', Oxford
Description: The tulips 'Kaiser Kroon' and 'Oxford' have a very delicate scent, and the two narcissi 'Carlton' and 'Fortune' are both strongly scented. The colour and scent of the florists' flowers, combined with the available garden material, make an interesting combination for the post-Christmas days of January, February and March.

Tulips and Narcissi

(Early in the year and Easter)

Container: A well made mahogany office desk tray from the late 1800s

Contents: Echeveria
Garrya elliptica catkins
Ivy
Narcissi
Tulips

Description: Suitable for a side table, this collection of reds, yellows and oranges harmonise well with the wooden container.

Magnolia and Arum Lilies

(Spring)

Container: Sheffield plate wine cooler

Contents: Arum Lilies: Zantedeschia aethiopica
Euphorbia characias
Magnolia soulangeana 'Alba'

Description: A combination of white and green material arranged with all their natural curves in a nineteenth century wine cooler of splendid proportions (see colour plate 3).

The magnolia and arum lilies are arranged much as they grow, each stem suggesting a certain position in the container, emphasising the importance of selecting and cutting. There is a great similarity in the substance of the petals of these two so very different flowers, thick textured, pure white and opaque. They are both long lasting, an important point to consider when planning flower arrangements for every day.

Tulips, Narcissi and Polyanthus
(Spring)
Arranged in a tea caddy for a country church window sill

Stage 1 (see opposite)
Fill the lining with crumpled wire netting, very firmly fixed, and then top up with water.
First arrange the crab apple branches and the sycamore, to form the basic structure of the group. Then place in position the first seven narcissi and the three tulips, as illustrated.

Stage 2 (see opposite)
At this point insert the remaining narcissi and tulips. Next the polyanthus, grouped as high as the stems will allow, at the back, and coming forward and over the front edge of the container, giving a rough informal appearance.

Stage 3 (see colour plate 4)
Now add the euphorbia and the polyanthus leaves, then the narcissus leaves, which should be inserted in bunches for preference rather than singly—a point always to remember. As a final touch add a few leaves of arum italicum.

Container: A Georgian Tea Caddy—a lining of decorative paper was often used for these caddies, in the present case it was of narrow striped yellow and gold wallpaper. Similar ones may be found, for small and large sums, in antique shops. A metal container, to hold the water, should be inserted inside the tea caddy.
Contents: Arum italicum
            Crab apple branches
            Euphorbia polychroma
            Narcissi, 'Cheerfulness', 'Carabineer'
            Polyanthus
            Sycamore
            Tulips, 'Ankara', 'Dillenburg'
Description: A Georgian tea caddy of dark mahogany with a mellow patina which only comes with advancing age. Nearly two hundred

Stage 1

Stage 2

years of dusting and polishing must give something that a contemporary wood cannot possibly possess.

A very good container for flowers, this tea caddy supports simple flowers from the garden in spring, ranging from cream to yellow, to peach, apricot and crimson to the bronze of the sycamore.

Early Spring into Summer

Whitsuntide

The flowers for Whitsuntide in St Albans Abbey are as always portraying the tongues of flame, which descended upon the Apostles, with their first teaching of the Christian religion (see colour plate 5).

So the colour red and as many variations of it as could be found at the time were used. My particular task was to arrange the flowers in a pedestal immediately in front of the lectern. Other members of the Abbey Flower Guild had white only to arrange, or red only, a wise move when two unrelated colours are to be used.

However, one can achieve a restful appearance by careful grouping—making sure that the dominant colour flows smoothly through the arrangement, as shown in this pedestal at St Michael and All Angels, Mill Hill.

Contents—red and white flowers:	
Carnations	Lilies
Gladioli	Peonies
Honesty	Philadelphus
Hosta leaves	Poppies
	Red Hot Pokers

Stage 1

Stage 2

Stage 3

Early Summer Arrangement in Cream and Lime Green Foxgloves, Lime

Container: Spanish Fruit Basket

Contents: Carnations
Foxgloves
Lime
Summer chrysanthemums, 'Esther Read', Hosta fortunei
albo-picta
Sweet peas

Description: A round wicker basket using stripped lime, foxgloves,

61

carnations, sweet peas, summer chrysanthemums: 'Esther Read', and Hosta fortunei albo-picta.

Soft pastel colours form the overall impression of the contents of this container.

The basket is loosely woven in natural split bamboo, round, with handles either side, made, not for flowers, but for fruit, and included in the price of the purchase of fruit in Spain. Its virtues far outweigh those of other baskets which are designed and fashioned for flowers. Very thin slithers of bamboo twisted over and over form the handles and the body is made in the usual way—the whole a warm straw colour.

With an oven dish and wire netting, the collection of material is our next concern.

With the two illustrations (see previous page) of the early stages of the development of the arrangement, it can quite clearly be seen how the the first steps are made.

I have said it before, but it can never be overstressed—how important is the choice of material used. The colour goes without saying but it is the line and flow of the branches and flowers giving the resultant graceful, comfortable appearance, which can either make or mar the group; these must be selected and cut with the container and its relative position in mind.

The choice of material for this basket in early summer is white and cream, shading to the palest primrose yellow of the carnations to the deeper soft yellow of the summer chrysanthemums.

To get a really lovely lime green effect at this time of the year, it is possible to use lime flowers and bracts stripped of their leaves, elder with their large flat green and white inflorescences stripped of their foliage, rhubarb flowers in tall stately spikes, hornbeam, too, stripped of its leaves, leaving the delightful lantern-like collections of bracts and seeds with a delicious scent. These and many others will give one the soft lime green, so useful to combine with flowers of pastel colouring.

Making my shape with the stripped lime, leaving only the lime green bracts and flowers on the stems, I formed a graceful outline, starting well back in the basket—in fact a good two thirds of the way back. Next I added the cream coloured foxgloves, cut to the required length, five stems to be precise. Next came the pastel yellow carnations, following the curves of the lime branches, and the palest yellow summer chrysanthemums. In the final stage, I put in the creamy-white sweet peas, starting high at the back of the group, coming forward and over to the left-hand side and down through the centre to the right-hand centre. Lime green hosta leaves, a lime green centre to the leaf and edges with a darker green, are invaluable for filling in low down, giving a clean look as the final touch.

Foxgloves and Roses

(Summer)

Container: Shallow rush basket

Contents: Digitalis purpurea, Foxglove—'Suttons' Primrose' and
'Sutton's Apricot'

Euphorbia lathyrus, Caper spurge

Hosta sieboldiana, Plantain lily

Lonicera periclymenum, Honeysuckle

Roses, Climber—'Dr van Fleet', 'Goldilocks', 'Albertine',
H.t. 'Sutters Gold'

Description: How important the word 'texture' is to all those
connected with interior decoration. The full value in both dull and
glossy textures is only appreciated when they are displayed together.

In this flower arrangement for the country church I have chosen a
shallow basket with a handle. The simple textured basket of cane and
rushes was made by hand. The framework and the handle are made of
a soft brown cane and the sides inset with plaited rushes.

The flowers and foliage I have used for this particular arrangement
could be obtained throughout the summer, June, July and August.
The side shoots of the foxgloves grow up just as soon as the main spike
is over and removed and for flower decoration purposes they are
invaluable with their gentle curves as they are so much lighter and
prettier. All the flowers and foliage in the basket have a very long
season so it is always possible to find a small quantity of each.

The simple garden flowers are well in keeping with the basket but the texture which lifts it from the all-over woolly appearance is the clean 'complexion' of the roses, a texture shared with many other flowers such as lilies, tulips, gladioli and many of the monocotyledons.

The overall colour of the arrangement is cream to yellow to peach and clear soft pink with lime green and glaucous green of the hosta. The scent should not be overlooked, especially as the hybridists of today are so concerned with the demand for scented roses. Those I have used in my arrangement are deliciously scented and the honeysuckle, we all know, never ceases to delight us.

The arrangement itself was made in an oven dish filled with wire netting and filled with water. Beginning at the back of the basket, the spurge is placed in position, then the foxgloves and honeysuckle. The right and left sides with flowing curves came next, then some of the hosta leaves near the centre, followed by the four varieties of roses placed well back and long, shortening towards the centre, only to lengthen again at the lowest point, namely the front and sides. The remainder of the hosta leaves give the group the final touch. A few adjustments here and there, a little filling in low down and the arrangement is complete.

This arrangement is planned to be viewed on a side table or chest, or window sill where the light falls on to it obliquely from above. In a dark church the colours of the flowers would light up well in artificial light and in a bright one they would look even more intense.

A Mid-Summer Group in White and Cream

Container: A mirror trough

Contents:

Artemesia. (1)

Cosmea. (2)

Dahlias. (3)

Dead nettle. (4)

Gladioli. (5)

Hedra canariensis variegata, Ivy. (6)

Margeurites. (7)

Molucella laevis, bells of Ireland. (8)

Nicotiana, white and green (9)

Onopordon. (10)

Phlox. (11)

Romneya coulteri. (12)

Roses: H.T. Virgo. (13)

Vinca major variegata, Periwinkle. (14)

Description: An asymmetrical arrangement, designed for a side altar using simple garden flowers and foliage.

There are many ways of using and enjoying white flowers and according to the colour of the background and foreground, so the flowers appear to change colour.

I particularly wanted to use garden flowers only for the arrangement illustrated here—flowers and foliage within the reach of most of us. The white cloth and grey background tend to intensify the whiteness of the flowers. As an experiment, place the same arrangement against a warm yellow background and notice the difference. The centres of the flowers which before appeared to be white are now green. Now change the lighting; a good north light will give you white flowers, warm sunshine cream flowers. A lot can be done, therefore, to enhance an arrangement of flowers by giving thought to background, foreground and lighting.

A fine white linen cloth and silver candlesticks with white candles complete the picture.

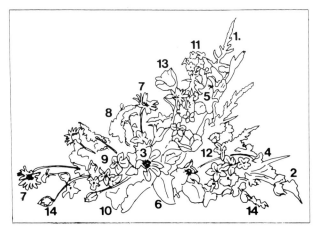

A Shallow Basket of Cane and Plaited Rushes, Lupins and Paeonies
(Early Summer)

An informal arrangement for the country church, carefully planned to be viewed below eye level. Placed on a low table, with its back to the wall, or pillar.

These subtle colours, closely related to each other, combine to make this an interesting group.

Stage 1

The tallest lupins and red hot pokers (Kniphofias) are put in place first, off-centre and to the back of the container. Then the long lupins and the weigela on the opposite side and the shorter stemmed material on the other side. The outline and shape of the group is now formed.

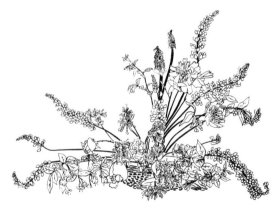

Stage 2

At this stage, the day lilies (Hemerocallis), some of the peonies, the roses and the honeysuckle, are added.

Stage 3

Now place in position the bearded iris and the hosta leaves—Hosta fortunei—and add the final touch by filling in the remaining spaces with honeysuckle and weigela.

Container: Shallow basket
Contents: Bearded iris
           Hemerocallis
           Honeysuckle
           Hosta fortunei
           Kniphofia
           Lupins
           Peonies
           Roses
           Weigela

Description: The flowers in the shallow basket are all related to each other by colour, blending also with the colour of the basket. Arranged as they are, in a casual way, the lupins taking on their own special shapes, giving a wonderful feeling of movement.

Autumn Arrangements

An Arrangement of Home-Grown Flowers

A most rewarding pedestal arrangement for church or home can be made up from plant material that is interesting to grow and absorbing to collect and arrange. The group illustrated here demonstrates the value of growing a collection of plants capable of producing background material for cutting with a very long season of availability (July to November if we have a mild autumn). This sort of plant material always looks good on its own, but can be doubly interesting if the last flowers of the season can be incorporated with it—the last dahlias, the last 'Peace' roses and the beautiful long stemmed sunflower Helianthus annuus 'Italian White', round which the whole

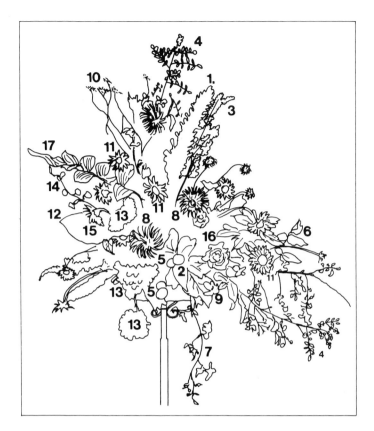

Contents: Acanthus mollis latifolius. (*1*)
Angelica archangelica. (*2*)
Atriplex hortensis cupreata. (*3*)
Bladder senna: Colutea arborescens. (*4*)
Chaenomeles japonica. (*5*)
Clematis heracleifolia davidiana 'Cote d'Azur'. (*6*)
Clematis tangutica. (*7*)
Dahlia. (*8*)
Euphorbia marginata. (*9*)
Fennel: Foeniculum vulgare. (*10*)
Helianthus annuus: 'Italian White'. (*11*)
Hosta fortunei (*12*)
Hydrangea. (*13*)
Nicandra physaloides. (*14*)
Nicotiana: 'Lime Green'. (*15*)
Rose: 'Peace'. (*16*)
Solomon's Seal: Polygonatum multi-florum. (*17*)

arrangement is built and which was the original inspiration for this group.

For those who are not already acquainted with this sunflower, it is a hardy annual growing four to five feet high with long lateral stems and small flowers of a very pale primrose-yellow with a dark bronze-brown centre. It is unexcelled for cutting and has a good long flowering season.

As a general rule a pedestal arrangement for a church should be placed well above eye level in order that it can still be enjoyed while the congregation is standing. This particular group could well be placed on the left of the chancel steps of a small church. Its highest point is to the left, with extra width to counter-balance this on the right. Starting at the back of the group is the light and graceful stem of bladder senna (Colutea arborescens). To the left of this is fennel (Foeniculum vulgare), and below this a Solomon's seal (Polygonatum multi-florum). Over to the right is a seed head of Acanthus mollis latifolius, the leaf of which has been the inspiration for artists in stone, wood, porcelain and silver right throught the ages since before Christian times in the great Roman and Greek empires.

Standing beside and in front of the acanthus is Atriplex hortensis cupreata, with the yellow foliage. To the centre and left are several heads of hydrangea—well mature and ready for drying. With stems split and placed in warm water in a warm room the heads will be dry and unshrivelled in about ten days.

The large leaves are those of Hosta fortunei and Angelica archangelica. Over to the right is another spray of colutea and Clematis tangutica, with its charming yellow bell-like flowers. To the centre and the side are yellow fruits of the quince: Chaenomeles japonica, and to the centre and right hand side the rough anemone-like leaves of Clematis heracleifolia davidiana 'Cote D'Azur'. The latter is an unusual semi-herbaceous species from China, with small hyacinth-like flowers. On closer inspection can be seen the useful Nicotiana 'Lime Green', Euphorbia marginata with the pale green bracts margined with white, and finally that hardy annual which is attractive in both flower and fruit, Nicandra physaloides.

A Collection of Dried and Preserved Subjects from the Garden and Hedgerow

Container: Copper saucepan—(see colour plate 16)
Contents: Acanthus
         Achillea
         Acroclinium
         Alchemilla mollis
         Allium

Amaranthus caudatus
Anaphalis triplinervis
Artemesia ludoviciana
Astilbe
Atriplex
Bracken
Cardoon
Delphinium
Dock (Sheep Sorrel)
Echinops
Eryngium alpinum
Eryngium tripartitum
Eryngium violetta
Fern
Gomphrena
Helipterum
Helichrysum
Hops
Hosta—seed heads
Hydrangea
Lime
Molucella—preserved in glycerine
Nicandra (Apple of Peru)
Old mans beard (Travellers Joy)
Rhodanthe
Roses
Whitebeam
Woad
Zea Mays gracillima variegata

Most of the seed-heads were tied in bundles and hung upside-down in an airy shed.

The whitebeam, beech, lime and molucella have been preserved in a solution of one-third glycerine to two-thirds water and left for three or four weeks and then dried. The garden fern was placed between two layers of newspaper under a carpet for a few weeks, then pressed with a warm iron and used as can be seen in the illustration.

Amongst the less usual plants for growing and eventually drying are acanthus and the red and green atriplex, the three eryngium and allium, nicandra and molucella.

The roses, in muted tones of their former glory, have been preserved in powdered borax, the hydrangea standing in shallow water in a warm room. A selection of all the material listed is shown in the illustration—a group which can give pleasure for many weeks during the winter.

A Grey Arrangement
(Mid-late Summer)
Container: Earthenware tazza

Description: What a wealth of colour there is at this time growing in the garden in the grey colour range. Grey-greens, grey-blues, grey-pinks and mauves, all these colours and more are shown in the above illustration

This group is arranged in an off-white tazza.

We have sung the praises of the hostas throughout the spring and the summer for their splendid leaves, the corrugated, the plain, the glaucous, the variegated, the twisted and the flat, but little has been said of their flowers. Arched spikes of soft mauve is the general description for them all, with slight variations in form and colour and height. An exception to this is one which I have used. The flowers of Hosta plantaginea, pure white and scented, are to the centre of the

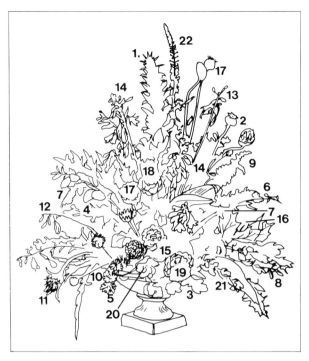

Contents: Acanthus latifolius. (*1*)
Allium cernuum. (*2*)
Aquilegia. (*3*)
Artemesia ludoviciana: (*4*)
Astrantia gracilis. (*5*)
Astrantia major. (*6*)
Buddleia davidii. (*7*)
Campanula. (*8*)
Ceanothus 'Gloire de Versailles'. (*9*)
Cineraria maritima. (*10*)
Cynara cardunculus: cardoon. (*11*)
Hosta crispula. (*12*)
Hosta lancifolia. (*13*)
Hosta plantaginea. (*14*)
Hosta undulata variegata. *15*)
Monarda fistulosa, bergamot/purple. (*16*)
Poppies: peony flowered. (*17*)
Roses: H.T. 'Sterling Silver', Floribunda 'Gletcher',
   'Lavender Lassie'. (*18, 19, 20*)
Sedum. (*21*)
Veratrum nigrum. (*22*)

arrangement. The taller ones at the top and sides were mostly cut from Hosta lancifolia, crispula and undulata variegata.

In order to whet the appetite of the gardeners, I have included a wide range of greys for growing in the ensuing years.

Flower arranging I find is an ever absorbing subject, especially when one is able to choose and cut unusual and interesting material. It is a subject from which one can never tire, as it is virtually impossible to do the same arrangement twice.

The group illustrated gave me plenty of scope for searching, cutting and arranging, in fact the whole operation was quite thrilling as it slowly developed.

Beginning at the back, I first placed in position in crumpled two inch wire netting, the Veratrum nigrum, an interesting flower spike with an even more interesting leaf, next came the acanthus and then the poppy flower and seed heads. Over to the left went the hosta flowers, the cardoon flower head and the allium. To the right an acanthus flower spike, a campanula, sedum and acanthus leaf. Running down through the centre is the Hosta plantaginea, Sterling Silver, with the delicious scent, Gletcher and Lavender Lassie, the delightful single flowered floribunda. To one side the astrantia and to the other a leaf of aquilegia, which always turns to an interesting purple at this time of the year.

An Arrangement of Roses from the Autumn Garden

I think I share with many horticulturists and ardent rosarians the thrill and joy of the last outdoor roses of the season. We are all aware that, given a mild autumn, roses continue to flower until Christmas. It is the ones that we are able to pick and use indoors in late September and October that possess a very special quality. The blooms have a certain lustre about them, the colours are clear, clean and subtle and the perfume, as ever, sheer delight.

A wrought iron pedestal is used for display (see colour plate 14) of the last available flowers of the herbaceous border and rose garden.

The Roses are: 'Colour Wonder'
　　　　　　　'Grandpa Dickson'
　　　　　　　'Pascali'
　　　　　　　'Sea Pearl'

The Herbaceous material:　　Nicotiana
　Decorative Kale　　　　　　Scabious
　Delphinium　　　　　　　　Verbascum
　Galtonia　　　　　　　　　Wild artemesia
　Lupin　　　　　　　　　　Wild clematis (Travellers Joy)

A few examples around Europe

Saint Saviour's Cathedral, Bruges, Belgium

According to legend, St Saviours Church was founded sometime about the year 640 by St Eloi, Bishop of Noyon. The same fate befell this church as did Notre Dame. The church has survived four fires only to be built and rebuilt again and again. When the diocese of Bruges was re-established in 1833-34 Saint Saviour's became Cathedral instead of the destroyed St Donatian's Cathedral.

The decoration on the altar consists of two carefully maintained growing cyclamen.

The central Chapel in the east end of the Cathedral is that of the Holy Sacrament. To the left of the Altar is a white marble statue of the Blessed Virgin by P. Pepers 1776 and two paintings by J. Van Oost, Senior, of Saint Peter and Saint John (see above photograph).

On the floor in front of the statue a well arranged vase of single and double spray chrysanthemums.

Saint Mary-le-Strand, London

Saint Mary-le-Strand built on an island site in Aldwych was the first major work of James Gibbs (1682–1754). In their Church brochure it says 'it displays a strong Italian baroque influence'—the reason being that the architect studied in Rome under Carlo Fontana, the papal architect. His later commissions include St Martin-in-the-Fields, the Radcliffe Camera at Oxford and the Senate House at Cambridge.

The Church constructed throughout of Portland stone has a three-tier steeple. Under the window hoods on the outside are fine carvings of cherubs and swags and panels of foliage and fruit around the apse.

The interior of the apse contains the holy name 'Jehovah' in Hebrew surrounded by cherubim and eucharistic symbols. The plaster work of the ceiling in the Italian style was in fact executed by two English craftsmen, Chrysoston and John Wilkins. The Royal Coat of Arms over the apse is that of George the First.

There has been a church standing on this site since 1143, when at that time Thomas à Becket, later Archbishop of Canterbury, was rector. In 1895 the Aldwych and Kingsway scheme, which took twenty-five years to complete, dramatically changed the character of the area.

As one walks down the steps into the unique and delightful little garden, planted with very interesting shrubs, hollies, magnolias and a pair of maidenhair trees: Ginko biloba under planted with Bergenia, one looks straight down the Strand to Trafalgar Square with Nelson's Column.

Close up flowers: Peach Gladioli, spray Chrysanthemum (St Mary-le-Strand)

Jerusalem

The Church of the Holy Sepulchre stands over Golgotha, the place of the Crucifixion and the tomb where the body of Jesus was laid. Since its first construction in AD 324 it has stood within the city walls only to be destroyed, rebuilt, destroyed and finally rebuilt by the Crusaders in the eleventh Century.

Marble vases of white iris on the altar, Church of the Holy Sepulchre, Jerusalem
Photo © Holyviews Ltd

Oslo, Norway

Oslo, a most interesting and beautiful city, is Norway's political, economic and cultural centre. The Cathedral at Stortorvet market place was built between 1694 and 1699. The exterior was restored in 1849–50, the interior in 1949–50. The altar piece is the original so too is the pulpit, dated 1699.

Oslo Cathedral: Simple flower arrangements in contrast to the ornate style of decoration
Photo © Mittet

Helsinki, Finland

The Rock Church—hewn from the hillside of solid granite near the centre of Helsinki:— was consecrated in September 1969. The Church is covered by a copper dome which is joined to the rock by reinforced concrete beams of various sizes, in between which there are 180 skylights (see colour plate 11).

The floor of the church is on the street level, designed so that the altar can be seen from the street through the glass doors. Its inner walls consist of bedrock and quarried stone and it has been left rough for acoustic and aesthetic consideration. Various kinds of coloured formations of rock add to the beauty of the walls, and in fact in one particular place the surface is brought to life by water running from cracks in the rock faces, which is led away through covered drains under the floor.

The altar table is made of smoothly sawn granite block, on which we found the assymetrical presentation of two candles on the right hand side of the altar and a vase of flowers on the left. The altar wall of the church is formed by an ice-age rock crevice and I am told that, during the summer months, sunlight falls against the altar during morning service.

St Paul's Anglican Church, Estoril, Portugal

The original church building was constructed in 1935 and was found to be adequate for the small congregation—however the numbers grew and grew, when thirty years later it was decided to rebuild the church some five times larger.

In 1967 the old building was knocked down, as it had been proved to be economically more advantageous to build a new church. On Christmas Eve of 1968 the first service was held at midnight.

The cross inside the church is made out of a tree from above the catacombs in Rome, where Priscilla, the first martyr died.

The clear glass windows of the porch, which are an interesting feature of contemporary design demonstrate the use of planting with attractive foliage plants in the garden outside.

The flowers are always beautifully maintained, simple and dignified, and befitting the design of this contemporary church.

The clear glass porch window showing the decorative plants growing outside: agapanthus, roses, fuchsia, poinsettia, hydrangea, creeper. St Paul's, Estoril, Portugal

PLATE 1
Contemporary Italian pottery shell, supported by dolphins, containing
winter flowering branches and flame 'Orange Triumph' Tulips (see
p 48).

PLATE 2

A brass preserving pan filled with late spring flowers – arranged above
eye level. The lower flowers in the pan are arranged in such a way that
they can be appreciated by the viewer standing below. The centre
flowers are looking forward while the flowers at the top are looking
upwards – so that the entire group looks good from any angle and any
distance. Contents: Azalea, Hosta leaves, Lilac, Lily-flowered tulip,
Pheasant Eye narcissi, Rhododendron, Tellima flowers.

PLATE 3
A spring arrangement of Magnolia and Arum Lilies in a nineteenth century Sheffield plate wine cooler (see p 57).

PLATE 4
Simple garden flowers – Tulips, Narcissi, Polyanthus – arranged in a
Georgian Tea Caddy for a country church window sill (see pp 58-59).

PLATE 5
St Albans Abbey. Lectern for Whitsuntide. Pedestal Arrangement.
Contents: Alstromeria, Carnations, Euphorbia, Hornbeam, Peonies,
Poppies, Roses, Stock (see p 60).

PLATE 6
Pedestal arrangement in the sanctuary beside the altar in St Clement
Danes church (see pp 109-111).

PLATE 7
An arrangement for a wedding in pastel colours at Brookmans Park
United Reformed Church, Hertfordshire. Contents: Bocconia, Carnations, Dahlias, Delphinium, Gladioli, Golden Rod, Hornbeam, Hydrangea, Nicotiana, Roses, Scabious, Verbascum.

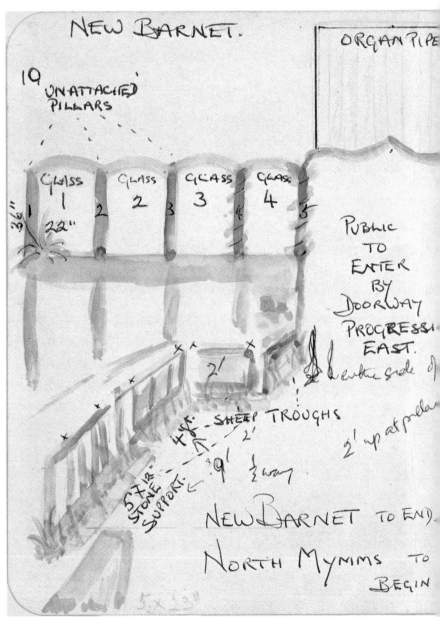

PLATE 8
Original sketches prepared before designing the arrangements for decorating the Choir area for a Flower Festival at St Albans Abbey (see p 101).

LIME GREENS —
WHITES
CREAMS
PALE YELLOWS.

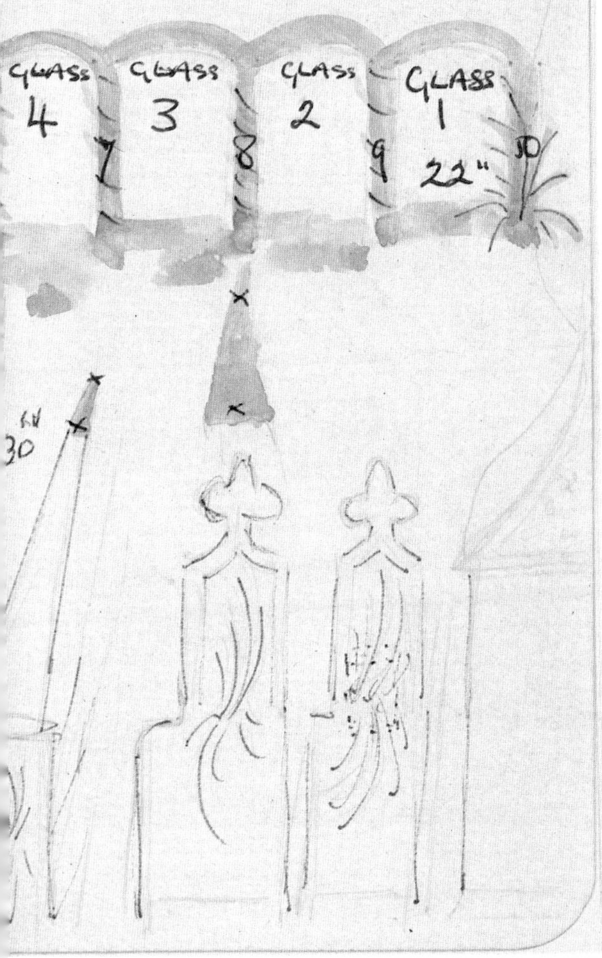

GLASS
4

GLASS
3

GLASS
2

GLASS
1

7

8

9

22"

10

6"
30

PLATE 9
Flowers and foliage used in this arrangement at the Bishop's Throne (see p 120) in St Albans: Alchemilla mollis, Allium siculum, Arum italicum, Arum lilies, Cardoon, Euphorbia, Onopordon, Sisyrinchium, Stripped hornbeam, White antirrhinum, White campanula, White carnations, White gladioli, Yellow antirrhinum, Yellow roses.

PLATE 10
Side Chapel with famous and valuable triptych with begonias in pots in full flower on the altar and in the side window. Hammerfest Church, Norway.

PLATE 11
The altar with its flowers of chrysanthemums, golden rod and zinnias. The Rock Church, Helsinki (see p 79). (*photo:* Hartyn D. Best).

PLATE 12
Haileybury and Imperial Service College Chapel with close up of an
arrangement at the Memorial Service for William Stewart, The Master
(see p 126).

PLATE 13
View looking towards the East windows in the Temple Church, City of London. In the Sanctuary and by the Wren reredos, was placed a small arrangement, by special request for the memorial of Lord Oaksey. (It might be of interest to architects and lovers of fine buildings to know that the pillars leading to the Sanctuary lean outwards naturally and are not a trick of the camera) (see pp 122-125).

PLATE 14
A formal pedestal arrangement in Autumn at North Mymms. Con-
tents: Artemesia; Atriplex; Decorative Kale; Delphinium; Galtonia;
Lupin; Nicotiana; Old-man's beard; Roses: 'Grandpa Dickson', 'Sea
Pearl', 'Pascali', 'Colour Wonder'; Scabious; Verbascum (see p 74).

PLATE 15
Harvest arrangement in a pad basket for porch window sill at Saint
Mary's Church, North Mymms. Contents: Apples on the branch,
Atriplex, Barley, Blackberry wild, Bronze hazel, Cardoon dried
flowers, Cauliflower leaves, Cotoneaster horizontalis, Dahlias, Elder
berries, Eleagnus, Fennel, Fern, Golden rod, Grapes white, Honesty,
Hydrangea, Ivy, Molucella.

PLATE 16
A collection of dried and preserved subjects from the garden and hedgerow in an autumn arrangement (see pp 70-71).

6
Flower Festivals

Planning

Planning a Flower Festival is quite an undertaking, but once the overall plans are formed in one's mind the sequence of events seem to follow in the correct order.

I begin to think out the plans about eighteen months ahead of the proposed month for the Festival.

The year 1965 saw the birth of the Flower Festival, an occasion lasting three to four days, where the church is decorated to a theme or colour scheme and which now many years later has become a very important social and fund raising event in parish and diocese alike.

My first Flower Festival in 1966 was to depict the rural industries of Hertfordshire. Working closely with the clergy, it was planned to be held at the time of the Patronal Festival of Saint Mary at the weekend, which according to the year, falls in the last week of June or the first week of July. Fortunately it is then high summer, when garden flowers are plentiful.

In the initial stages I find a Committee of one is the easiest way to plan the event!

I visit the church many times taking measurements of window sills, choir stalls, altar rails, niches, pulpit and lectern, font and spaces where pedestal arrangements may be used. Following this I make the mental plans of the overall designs—draw up the list of Flower Clubs and Parishioners who will be invited to take part and a few individuals from near and far who indirectly draw friends, relations and members of their own Flower Club, thereby adding to the number of visitors who come to view the church. All the children of schools in the Parish are invited to take part—the Font is a favourite site for the little ones to work with help from their own teachers.

By September of the year before the Festival a committee has been formed, each member taking on special duties—the Chairman keeping a watchful eye on everyone and delegating such duties as Secretary, Treasurer, parking and site managers, publicity and catering. I find myself a Secretary, the first letter is drafted out, hopefully approved by all and signed by the Vicar and myself and posted in mid September. Never expect answers by return for the obvious reason that some people are still on holiday and the Flower Clubs may have had a meeting the night before and therefore cannot give a firm answer for four weeks, until their next monthly meeting.

The next letter follows in about mid October giving each society or individual the position where they will be working, enclosing a ground plan of the church, with notes of colours of stained glass windows and measurements, a list of titles which make up the theme. This letter should go out in time for all to choose their subject, long before Christmas intervenes, giving a second choice too, so in fact those who answer first will get their first choice.

I have always had one particular person as a personal assistant to make sure that all goes smoothly in the event of an accident to myself. Garden flowers and foliage, where possible are mentioned in the letter, so too are travelling expenses and extra bought flowers, as many decorators like to use the flowers of their choice, bound only by the necessary colour scheme. I then wait for the replies to this letter. The third letter goes out telling each member of the team their final choice, confirming the position and colour scheme, also to tell them that refreshments at mid-morning, lunch time and tea will be provided. A Sub Treasurer is on duty all the day of staging so that those who wish can claim their expenses in cash. This saves many letters and postage after the event. All staging is to be completed and the church completely tidied up by 5 pm as that evening a service of dedication is held, after which the congregation may wander round and enjoy the Festival.

Publicity and Catering are extremely important, the former where we circulated every Church within a twenty mile radius, suggesting Coach parties, the London Hotels had posters enticing foreign visitors—the handbills included the rose garden and parkland of North Mymms Park and the temptation of Cream Teas. Car stickers were issued a little later for all of us to advertise the Flower Festival. About a week before the Festival handbills were put through every door in the parish, advertising and reminding everyone of the date, time and place and facilities for parking.

Posters advertising the Flower Festival were distributed to Shops and Libraries and Churches nearby and those mounted on boards and covered with polythene to protect them from the rain, were displayed with permission of course, on all roadsides approaching the Parish, but here lies the very important difference. Place them—perhaps in threes—for if you have ever tried to read a poster when you are driving a car—it is virtually impossible to do so. Therefore display them perhaps twenty yards apart in sets of three—the first one fixes the particular church of . . . the second, at a glance one can read the dates and the third the times of the church being opened. On a busy road it is extremely difficult to slow down and sometimes impossible to stop, so here lies our well planned and successful experiment.

On the morning of preparation for the Flower Festival, there ready for all to use are buckets of foliage, flowers, garden or bought, well conditoned and placed in deep cold water, wire netting two inch mesh, oasis, cloths, spare buckets, dust sheets, small and large watering cans, kitchen steps, folding step ladders and ladders. Good strong nylon fishing line around the 40 pound breaking strain, for hanging lanterns of flowers from pillar or beams. Dustpans, brushes, brooms and quantities of water readily available.

For the designer, director, be for ever on the spot with advice where requested—physical help if needed and to be permanently calm.

Many churches now charge an entry fee to view the church, however in the early days of Flower Festivals we had large glass carboys at the West end where contributions were collected. A small sum was charged for parking cars and coaches. Admission to the famous gardens of the Park was gained by paying on entry.

This may all sound very commercial, in fact it is, for apart from the pleasure one hopes to give, the whole operation is conducted in the nicest possible way to raise as much money as one can for, perhaps, the church roof, the tower, the organ or for what is most needed. Some smaller amounts are given to needy charities.

During each day of the Flower Festival a team of people is needed to fill up every arrangement, right to the top, with water, twice daily and if it is very hot weather to spray every group of flowers with a fine mist of cold water. A quantity of spare flowers, kept in a cool cellar, can be used to replace any flower which wilts.

That first Festival in 1966 raised the grand total of one thousand guineas!

Through the ensuing years I have been invited to take part in the decoration for various charities of country churches, town and city churches, schools and college and university chapels, cathedrals and stately homes in town and country.

St Mary's, North Mymms, Hertfordshire.

North Mymms Parish Church

In the year 1965 I began to plan for the first Flower Festival at Saint Mary's Church, North Mymms—my own Parish Church. It was to be a three day event and decorated to the theme of the Rural Industries of Hertfordshire—Basket weaving, furniture making, wrought iron work, with of course the spinning of real silk from the silkworms at Ayot St. Lawrence and many more. All the pedestal arrangements, of which there were ten, were shaded from white and cream in the sanctuary through to peach, pink, blue, pink and purple, to deep clashing reds at the west door and exit. Visiting Flower Arrangement Societies from a radius of ten miles took part, and visitors came from far and wide to this first ever Flower Festival of 1966.

One of the first considerations in the planning is to set down some notes about the church and its special features. (See example on pages 85, 87, 91, also see colour plate 8.)

84

Notes on the Parish Church of Saint Mary North Mymms, Hertfordshire

History

The first reference to our Parish Church occurs in Domesday Book in 1086 where the area of North Mymms was then the property of Robert, Bishop of Chester.

MIMMINE as it was then known and according to the records it is safe to assume that there was a church with a manor house nearby.

The next recorded date is 1237 and by that time there must have been a more permanent building, for in that year, Thomas de St Albans was instituted vicar of North Mymms. His little church was probably on the site of St Katherine's Chapel and some authorities are of the opinion that parts of his church are incorporated in the present chancel walls.

Architecture

The present church as it now stands was the plan of Simon de Swanland, a wealthy London merchant who acquired the manor of North Mymms in 1316. Within twelve years he had built a chantry chapel, dedicated it to St Katherine, and endowed it for the maintenance of a priest. Another twelve years went by and his plans for a large church with transepts and central tower were being modified. Traces of these plans are to be seen in the heavy construction of the chancel arch and the filled-in arch in the east wall of the south aisle. It is thought that the tower was built between 1430 and 1450.

The tower contains a peal of eight bells, the peal of which the ringers and their captain are justly proud.

Furniture and Ornaments

The Church plate, some dating back to the Elizabethan period is of great interest to the parish and visitors. It includes a silver cup made in London 1568/9, a silver flagon of 1707, a pair of chased lidded chalices of 1614 and many other beautiful pieces of church silver. The most unusual possession is the unique Amber Tankard, made in Nuremburg in 1659. The panels of amber, set in silver-gilt, are carved with female figures representing the Virtues and such is its rarity that it is on permanent loan, with the British Museum.

A handsome oak board in the porch bears the names of the vicars since Thomas de St Albans was instituted in 1237.

The most recent addition to the Church in the 1960s is the new kneelers, the design, the tapestries and their making up have been carried out by ladies of the parish over a period of four years.

Festival themes

After a three year interval, in 1969 another financial and great social success was recorded at North Mymms; the theme I chose, for the entire design throughout the Church, was Classical Music titles. A most rewarding and pleasurable Festival to direct. Yet another interval of three years and in 1972 saw the third Flower Festival. The theme for the Flower Decoration Societies on this occasion was taken from the Book of Common Prayer: the cantile *Benedicite Omnia Opera*, 'Oh ye works of the Lord, Bless ye the Lord.' Demonstrations of Well Dressing by skilled people from Derbyshire and brass rubbings by our own parishioners, the concerts in the church, and the opening of the famous grounds and gardens of Mrs Evelyn Burns and Major General Sir George Burns KCVO, CB, DSO, OBE, MC, Lord Lieutenant of Hertfordshire, make this large parish with the small church one of the most active societies in the county.

In 1976 saw our fourth Festival of Flowers, where each society chose a 'Treasure of the Earth' depicting Diamonds, Jade, Garnets, Coal and Oil, Mother O'Pearl and Coral and many many others—each one a flower arranger's dream—such lovely colours to work with at the end of June and beginning of July. Each visiting society and individual chose the treasure of their choice under my direction and design as previous Festivals, my plans were made over a period of ten months. The hand painted sketches (see pages 94–95) give a clear basic design for arrangements: for the East window sill, the pedestal either side of the altar, the alternative designs for the altar rail, and finally in sanctuary and chancel, the suggested 'sheaves' of flowers for the stall ends of the clergy. The last design shown is for a south facing window with clear glass, flowing lines on a four foot four inch wide sill, and seventeen inches deep. The left arrangement to be larger than the right.

Saint Mary's Church, lying as it does in parkland, and far from the community it serves, at morning service is packed to the doors with young and old. A strong feeling of belonging is very much in evidence and truly felt by all denominations.

A wonderful fellowship of ladies exists and their assistance is seen and felt throughout the parish. The decorations of the church with flower arrangements for Festivals of the Church Calendar, and weddings and in fact 'everyday' are always beautifully maintained.

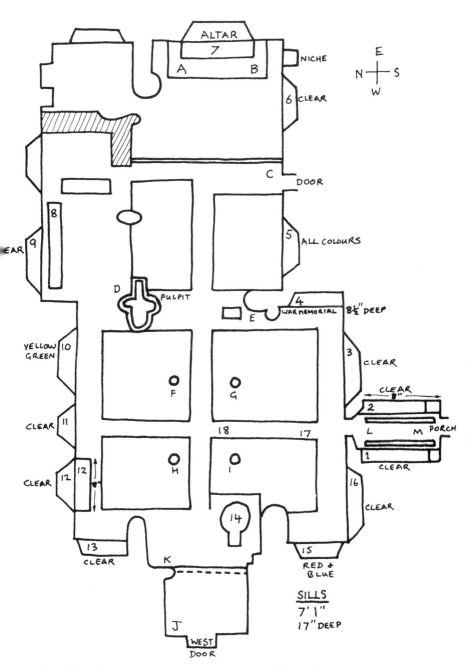

Plan of North Mymms church showing areas designated to the different Flower Clubs (by numbers) and position of large pedestals (by letters). Measurements of sills and colour of windows are also given.

87

Suggested Themes for Flower Arrangements within the Festival theme 'Classical Music Titles'

MENDELSSOHN	*'The Italian'*
MOZART	*Clarinet Concerto*
BIZET	*Carmen*
HANDEL	*Water Music*
HOLST	*The Planets*
MUSSORGSKY	*Pictures at an Exhibition*
RIMSKY-KORSAKOV	*Scheherazade*
SCHUBERT	*'The Unfinished Symphony'*
DVORAK	*'The New World'*
ELGAR	*Enigma Variations*
MENDELSSOHN	*Fingals Cave*
MOZART	*Eine Kleine Nachtmusik*
OFFENBACH	*Orpheus in the Underworld*
WAGNER	*'The Flying Dutchman'*
PUCCINI	*Madam Butterfly*
BEETHOVEN	*'The Pastoral'*
CHOPIN	*Les Sylphides*
TCHAIKOVSKY	*Swan Lake, Sleeping Beauty, Romeo and Juliet*
SAINT-SAENS	*Carnival of the Animals*
STRAVINSKY	*Rites of Spring*
LIZST	*Hungarian Rhapsodies*
BEETHOVEN	*Moonlight Sonata*

Groups in the Sanctuary, St Mary's North Mymms, arranged by members of the parish for the first flower festival in 1966. Displayed to right and left is the antique silver and in the centre the amber tankard.

One of a pair of my wall decorations used on either side of the south door within the porch at North Mymms for the 'Classical Music Titles' Festival in 1969. Living flowers, foliage, fruit and vegetables, with dried seed heads, ribbons and musical instruments were grouped together with a thumb-nail picture showing the montage work designed to advertise the Flower and Music Festival, (see programme cover on right) using music, a rose, a bust of Bach, a violin, trumpet and a flower arrangement.

Design carried through onto programme cover for 'Classical Music Titles' Festival.

From:- **BENEDICITE, OMNIA OPERA**

(handwritten: North Mymms)

(handwritten: Wiesfield Hill) O all ye Works of the Lord, bless ye...

(handwritten: New ...) O ye Angels of the Lord, bless ye...

(handwritten: Tottenage) O ye Heavens, bless ye...

O ye Waters that be above the Firmament, bless ye...

O all ye Powers of the Lord, bless ye...

(handwritten: Harpenden) O ye Sun and Moon, bless ye... ✓

O ye Stars of Heaven, bless ye...

(handwritten: Mid Herts) O ye Showers and Dew, bless ye... *(handwritten: WINDOW sill)*

(handwritten: Enfield) O ye Winds of God, bless ye...

(handwritten: Potters Bar) O ye Fire and Heat, bless ye... ✓

(handwritten: Southgate) O ye Winter and Summer, bless ye...

(handwritten: North ...) O ye Dews and Frosts, bless ye...

(handwritten: North ...) O ye Frost and Cold, bless ye... ✓

(handwritten: C Range ...) O ye Ice and Snow, bless ye... *(handwritten: WRITE TO MRS COATS. 7–14lbs Glass offered & accepted.)*

(handwritten: Cuffley) O ye Nights and Days, bless ye... ✓

(handwritten: Wheathampstead 15) O ye Light and Darkness, bless ye... ✓

~~O ye Light and Darkness, bless ye...~~

O ye Lightnings and Clouds, bless ye...

(handwritten: Welham Green) O ye Mountains and Hills, bless ye...

(handwritten: Church School) *(handwritten: St Albans)* O all ye Green Things upon the Earth, bless ye... ✓

(handwritten: Hatfield) O ye Wells, bless ye... ✓

(handwritten: Hatfield) O ye Seas and Floods, bless ye... ✓

(handwritten: Hatfield) O ye Whales, and all that move in the Waters, bless ye... ✓

(handwritten: Welham ...) O all ye Fowls of the Air, bless ye...

(handwritten: Greenwich Church School) O all ye Beasts and Cattle, bless ye... ✓

From my working notes for the North Mymms 1972 Flower Festival.

From the Festival brochure,
North Mymms, 1976

Flower Festival

2nd, 3rd and 4th JULY 1976

Parish Church of St. Mary

NORTH MYMMS

Hertfordshire

How to get to the Festival

The above map shows the position of the Festival, close to the A.1., near Hatfield. Motorists should have no difficulty, as approach roads are first class and the site will be well sign-posted.

The nearest railway stations are Hatfield and Brookmans Park on the Kings Cross main line, and the nearest underground is High Barnet on the Northern Line. Buses from these stations pass the Festival entrance. Bus routes which will serve the Festival site are the 716A Green Line from Marble Arch, and the 343 connecting Welwyn, St. Albans, Dunstable and Brookmans Park.

Please show this brochure to your friends as we are anxious to welcome as many visitors as possible.

Festival Enquiries to
B. E. TURBERVILLE,
38 THE GARDENS,
BROOKMANS PARK,
HATFIELD, HERTS.
Telephone Potters Bar 57904

Concert Box Office:
D. R. HYDE,
24 THE GARDENS,
BROOKMANS PARK,
HATFIELD, HERTS.
Tel. Potters Bar 55209
please enclose S. A. E.

Frontispiece
designed and photographed by GODFREY BEST, A.I.I.P.

Photograph of
House by W. T. FIELD — Church by GODFREY BEST,
A.I.I.P.

From the Festival brochure,
North Mymms, 1972.

"TREASURES OF THE EARTH"

AMBER	LEAD
ALABASTER	LIMESTONE
AQUAMARINE	(MOTHER O'PEARL
AMETHYST	(PEARL
BRONZE	MARBLE
BERYL	OPAL
BRASS	PERIDOT
CAIRNGORM	PEWTER
COPPER	PLATINUM
COAL	RUBY
CORAL	SAPPHIRE
CHALCEDONY	SANDSTONE
DIAMOND	SERPENTINE
EMERALD	SLATE
GARNET	SILVER
GOLD	SARDONYX
IRON	TOPAZ
JADE	TIN
JASPER	TURQUOISE
LAPIS LAZULI	ZIRCON

*From my working notes of the list of themes for the North Mymms 1976
Flower Festival 'Treasures of the Earth'.*

Preliminary sketches for arrangements in North Mymms

Sketch 1. *Diagram shape of arrangements for East Window with glass of blues and mauves.*

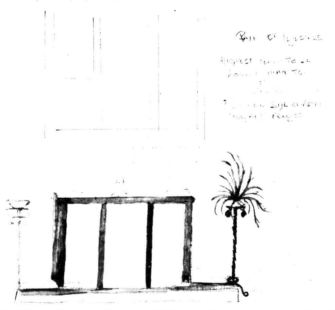

Sketch 2. *Diagram for pair of pedestals where highest point of arrangement to be lower than top of cross.*

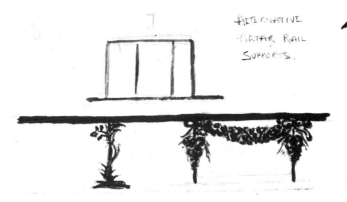

Sketch 3. *Diagram for alternative arrangements for altar rail supports.*

Sketch 4. *Diagram for arrangements on ends of clergy stalls.*

Sketch 5. *Diagram for suggested shapes of arrangements for a clear glass South Window measuring 4 ft 4 in wide, and approx 17 in deep.*

Finchley Methodist Church

From about the turn of the century this well proportioned red brick church has stood in an increasingly busy thoroughfare—in fact on the direct route from South Hertfordshire to London.

It is a very active Church, serving the community in every possible way.

The interior, with its panelled walls surrounding the altar is light, colourful and inviting.

During an autumn Flower Festival entitled 'The Crown of the Year' I was invited to take part in decorating the Church. It was planned for the enrichment of all, and over a period of two days many hundreds of people, who were inspired and enchanted, passed through the church.

A pedestal arrangement beside the holy table in Finchley Methodist Church. White and lime green are the predominant colours in the group—which stand out so well against the polished wood background. The flowers included in the group are gladioli, white carnations, acidanthera—(the small, sweetly scented spiked flower found in Abyssinia).

Dahlias, single spray chrysanthemums, nicotiana 'lime green' and nicotiana white, euphorbia wulfenii (green flowers). Amaranthus (green love-lies bleeding). Phytolacca (green flowers and unripe berries). Angelica (green seed head). Ivy, hops, romneya coulteri (grey foliage).

97

Saint Albans Cathedral/Abbey Church

A building of austere majesty set on the top of a hill in Hertfordshire, Saint Albans Abbey is one of the largest of the English cathedral churches. It was built by the Normans, who were the greatest builders of their time.

According to recent research into old manuscripts, it seems fairly certain that the martyrdom of Alban took place in AD 209. He was beheaded for his interest in the Christian faith. Over a century later when Christianity was accepted by the Roman emperors it is thought that the very first shrine was built on the place of execution and dedicated to St Alban.

During the eleventh century the Abbey was rebuilt using the Roman bricks which were at hand from the demolished buildings of Verulamium, the Roman town. The thin, tile-like bricks of the Romans proved to be invaluable.

So many of our mediaeval cathedrals are constructed of local rock in the form of limestone or sandstone but the county of Hertfordshire is poorly supplied with natural stone apart from flint, however this being the only local hard material it is used to face the exterior walls.

St Albans became a seat of learning in the late ten hundreds where monks were engaged in copying books. The House flourished and it was during the Norman period that the monastic school was first mentioned in the records: it has survived through many changes to become today the famous St Albans School for Boys.

So much of the middle life of the Abbey can be studied from the book compiled by Mr Geoffrey Jarvis entitled *The Story of St Albans Abbey*—which enables me to reach the present day—where in 1875 a Bill was passed through Parliament making the Abbey the cathedral of a new diocese which covered Hertfordshire and Essex—now Hertfordshire and Bedfordshire. In 1877 Thomas Legh Claughton was enthroned as the first Bishop of St Albans. Now in the twentieth century St Albans Abbey—a large building of great historical interest and religious significance, attracts many pilgrims and sightseers. In 1977 the ninth centenary of Paul de Caen, the first Norman Abbot was celebrated by a Festival of Flowers in an act of thanksgiving. I had the honour and indeed thrill to work alongside three others as the Design Committee. The planning for such an enormous undertaking took no less than eighteen months under the inspiration and leadership of the Fraternity of Friends of the Abbey.

My final work was to design and organise the decoration of the Choir, the Bishop's throne, with the Chaplain's stall and finally my individual work of a matching pair of pedestal arrangements either side of the High Altar.

An undulating border of flowers arranged in sheep troughs beneath the choir stalls. On the corner of each stall is an asymmetrical group for a Flower Festival in St Albans Abbey.

Side view of stalls, in St Albans Abbey, showing sheaves of flowers.

The Bishop's Throne and Chaplain's Stall, St Albans Abbey, with flowers at the base, and finely made garlands of foliage twined around the carved pillars.

I chose to have the decoration in lime greens, whites, creams and pale yellows. The teams to do the work of decorating it were my own Flower Decoration Society—North Mymms Floral Art Group, New Barnet Floral Art Society, Saint Mary's North Mymms and Haileybury College. At the High Altar with its reredos made of elaborate carvings in stone, I wanted the flowers to be a highlight in such a vast expanse, so in order that they would show up well, I chose mixed reds, scarlet, purple, orange red gladioli, roses and carnations.

There were just under 200 arrangements ranging from modest posies by children, to vast constructions in shaded colours, from the West end the Nave Altar and beyond. Every parish, every Flower arrangement society, many schools, nurserymen, parks, The Royal National Rose Society, The Fraternity of Friends of the Abbey, all worked together as a mighty diocese on the day of staging. The result was breathtaking. Thousands of people enjoyed the great spectacle and the result was a great social and financial success.

Decoration plan: the Choir

From the original sketch (see colour plate 8) it can be seen that I divided the Choir into equal halves for the two flower clubs to do their decorations.

Immediately placed under the organ pipes is a screen through which the choir progresses and for the days of the Festival, a route for the public to follow, carefully worked out and marked with arrows.

The screen with eight glass panels supported by ten free standing fine wooden pillars, divides the choir from the choir vestry.

Round these pillars were wound very finely made garlands of foliage, with a group of lime green with lemon yellow flowers either end. The choir stalls had a small arrangement at each end marked by an X.

At the foot of the stalls marked five feet twelve inches and four feet matched on the other side by the same arrangements, are sheep troughs borrowed from a local farmer, filled with well soaked Oasis and topped with a layer of two inch wire netting.

Stripped lime, stripped hornbeam, alchemilla, hosta, bergenia and eleagnus were some of the foliages that were used, with gladioli, roses, golden rod, keeping as near to garden flowers as we could.

Bishop's Throne

As can be seen in the photograph (see p. 100) the pillars of the Bishop's Throne, arranged by Haileybury College, were entwined with a delicate garland, a trough below, continuing the design of the undulating bank of flowers. To the left of the Throne can be seen a bank of flowers built upon a construction: a wooden frame on to which several metal containers are fixed, in order to have flowers from floor to the height required (see p. 120).

7
Arrangements for Special Occasions

Baptism

A decoration for the top of the font is a lovely way to welcome a very new life into the Church.

I have in the past been asked to do an arrangement of perhaps pastel coloured flowers on a pedestal in the baptistry with no further decoration, or alternatively to make a 'font top'. This can be made on a circular frame on which is bound wet moss. On to which is pinned separate pieces of green 'bun' moss. Simple garden flowers, like violets, snowdrops, primroses, miniature roses, daisies are mounted in an uneven number of separate groups, five or seven, according to the size of the font and frame, with the addition of delicate foliage.

The font illustrated (see opposite) has excellent proportions, is made of cream coloured stone and is found in Christ Church, Little Heath, Hertfordshire, a church built at the turn of the century.

Plan for a Font top arrangement

A Necklace for a Baby Girl

Given the right ingredients, that is, a baby girl dressed in a long, conventional christening gown for her baptism, there is nothing I enjoy more than making a very fine necklace (see sketch above) on pink baby ribbon—with perhaps white and pink carnation petals used alternately with pink edged daisies from the lawn or miniature roses.

There are many ways of decorating a font for a baptism, and the one I have chosen is my favourite. The simple garden flowers, available in the autumn were: Euonymous radicans variegata; Tiny Pink Roses: Cécile Brunner; Variegated Ivy; White and Lilac coloured Colchicum; White and Pink Cyclamen neapolitanum.

Weddings

When planning the flowers for a wedding, be it country church, school chapel, town or city church or cathedral, my personal plans are precisely the same as for the Flower Festivals. Having discovered the bride's preference of colour schemes and the colour of the bridesmaids dresses, then one can advise on the flowers in season and the most suitable places for the arrangements to be displayed.

The bride and bride's mother usually know exactly where they wish to have the flowers. Some like a very simple wedding with garden flowers. They very often choose to have a pedestal arrangement beside the altar, perhaps another at the chancel steps, a bowl on a table at the West end and a larger group in the porch to give a good welcome. Others prefer something a little more sophisticated, with more formal arrangements and more exotic flowers, with perhaps arrangements on the pew ends, with garlands of foliage and flowers at the altar rail.

Bouquet for a Bride— made with Roses, 'Virgo', Freesia, Cobaea scandens, Chlorophytum, Fern, and Tradescantia.

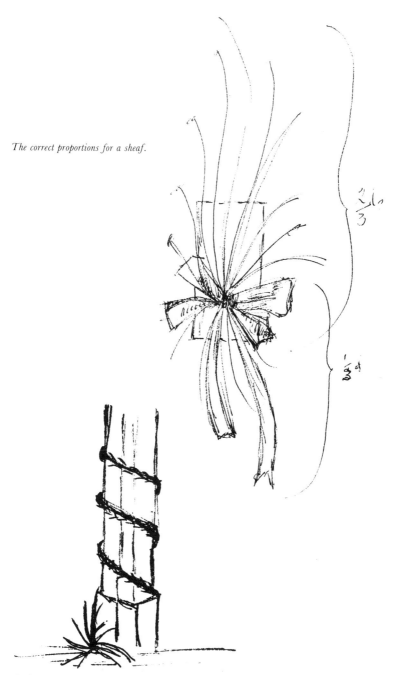

The correct proportions for a sheaf.

$\dfrac{2}{3}$

$\dfrac{1}{3}$

Garland of evergreen foliage round a pillar.

Garlands of evergreen foliage can be made on lengths of thick string or cord—by cutting pieces of foliage in two inch lengths and binding them on piece by piece with binding wire to the cord. If flowers are to be added, then spaces should be left at regular intervals, where small pieces of oasis, well soaked in water and carefully wrapped in very thin polythene can be added. It is a wise move to measure the pillar, or support before beginning the work, for as the garland is wound round the pillar it will be found that the length is once and a half times the measurement of the pillar.

Sheaves are simple to make and very decorative for perhaps the supports of altar rails, the ends of choir and clergy stalls, and pew ends.

By wrapping a well soaked piece of oasis in polythene, then surrounded with wire netting, it can be placed flat on a table for working.

The overall proportions of a sheaf are very important, for unlike a table centre, where the centre is in the middle, a sheaf to be really accurate should be divided into thirds, so that the top is two-thirds and the lower part one third, as can be seen in the sketch (on previous page). Larger flowers, perhaps three roses, as we say 'on the move' added to the centre give the design an important point to which the eye should be drawn. Bows of ribbon, made up of two loops mounted on wires, placed in the centre with two long ends hanging from the returned end. There are various ways of hanging them up, with two wires therefore giving us four ends to twist tightly together. Fishing line, which is extremely strong and damages nothing, and perhaps a piece of 'Blue Tak' to stick to the woodwork at the bottom of the sheaf. When the ceremony is over all can be removed, the 'Blue Tak' leaving no mark at all. Good quality ribbon, wide enough to make important bows, give an extra boost to a festive occasion.

Queenswood School, Hatfield, Hertfordshire

Queenswood School for the education of girls on the same lines as the public schools for their brothers was the conception of two enterprising Methodist Ministers in the Victorian Age of 1894.

Its birth took place in a capacious family mansion in King's Road, Clapham Park, London. Thirty years later in 1924 when the school had outgrown its accommodation in King's Road, the transfer to Hatfield was made. In this lovely woodland spot, called Queenswood, the second act in the history of the School begins. The part of the School which is relevant to this particular account is of course the Chapel built in the ensuing ten years. In character with the rest of the

Queenswood School Chapel, Hatfield.

estate, the chapel is built of red brick, with high windows which give excellent daylight. A simple, plain altar at the East end of the chapel, is always decorated with the most beautiful flowers grown and cut from the private gardens. On the South side behind the choir stalls can be seen the organ, and on either side of the chapel a pair of carved wooden pulpits can be seen.

It has long been a privilege of past pupils, that they can return to be married at the place where they lived and worked for several years of their early life.

A large group placed in one of the two pulpits of Queenswood School Chapel, for the wedding of a
past pupil. The container is a copy of a Georgian wine cooler, filled with flowers, berries and foliage of
early autumn. Unripe berberis berries, variegated ivy, snowberry and angelica leaves form the outline;
while white spray chrysanthemums, white bloom chrysanthemums, dahlias, hydrangea and carnations
form the main decoration. All the flowers in white, cream and apricot were chosen to blend with the
predominate colours of the long dresses of the bridesmaids.

St Clement Danes, Church of the Royal Air Force

As far back as the year 886 and before, a place of worship has stood on the site in Aldwych known as Saint Clement Danes. The invading Danes of that time found it a fair place to settle. Many were driven out by Alfred the Great but those who had married English women and were residing in London were allowed to live between Westminster and Ludgate—they built an house of worship which was consecrated and called St Clement Danes. The Danes being sea-faring men dedicated the church to Saint Clement, an early bishop of Rome and patron saint of mariners.

Although the original church building was not damaged in the Great Fire of London of 1666 it was fast falling into disrepair and by 1668 it had to be pulled down and rebuilt.

At that time Sir Christopher Wren was at the height of his genius and powers, he undertook to design and supervise the building of a new church on the island, in the Strand, and he raised the beautiful building we see today, except for the steeple which was designed and added by James Gibb in 1719.

In the eighteenth century prosperity returned and this particular parish was then a fashionable part of London, to it came such famous writers of the time, Addison, Congreve, Steele, Johnson, Goldsmith and Gay and a little later Charles Lamb. The immortals of the theatre—Sheridan, Garrick and Keane rubbed shoulders with the famous artists Hogarth, Reynolds and Romney.

St Clement Danes, Church of the Royal Air Force as it is now known, is a very handsome building—the interior is very beautiful indeed, in fact very striking. Dark, black oak predominates up to the height of the gallery. Above, all is brightness and light, white, grey and gold.

The panelled ceiling is supported by elegant columns and the whole is enhanced by the richly flowing colours of the Stuart arms. Below is the strikingly wide aisle which stretches the length of the church like a carpet of stone. This is an impression largely due to the ingenuity of the architect who made the pews telescopic.

The flower arrangements illustrated (see colour plate 6, and pp. 110–111) were made for a wedding in the month of October. They are useful in illustrating shape and texture of plant material.

The groups all contain foliage and flowers in the lime green, white, cream, lemon yellow through to the slightly warmer shade of yellow of the rose 'Roselandia.'

An arrangement in the sanctuary at St Clement Danes Church for an October wedding (see opposite for contents).

The material includes:
Cardoon. (1)
Carnations: pale lemon, white
Chrysanthemum: Tokyo, white single spray.(2)
Crocosmia
Dahlias white. (3)
Gladioli, white and yellow. (4)
Helichrysum. (5)
Hornbeam. (6)
Hydrangea. (7)
Lilies: L. auratum, L. 'Yellow Limelight'. (8, 9)
Roses: 'Iceberg', 'Roselandia', 'Tiara',

111

Christ Church Cathedral Church, Oxford

'That sweet City with her dreaming spires'. One of the best known literary references to Oxford by the nineteenth century poet, Matthew Arnold. Although many colleges were founded and built in the middle of the thirteenth century, the sky line remains very much the same today in the twentieth century.

The University of Oxford is made up of a large number of colleges all of which have been established separately and at different times. In

The choir and high altar of Christ Church Cathedral, Oxford. The pillars are Norman whilst the delicate fan vaulting dates from the fifteenth century. A large flower arrangement is placed on the north side of the altar for an autumn wedding.

Within Christ Church Cathedral, Oxford, near the West door is the fine wooden screen, against which were placed a matching pair of arrangements giving an instant welcome to the bridal party. A leaden urn placed on a joint stool with flowers, foliage and seed heads to complement those of the sanctuary.

Contents: Bracken

Carnations

Chrysanthemums:

Bloom

Rayonnante

Spray

Gladioli

Old Man's Beard

A good sturdy plinth supporting an urn of lead, well in proportion with the vast and spacious sanctuary of Christ Church Cathedral, Oxford.

Contents: Bracken, dried and pressed
          Carnations, peach and apricot
          Chrysanthemums:
              Bronze, single spray
              Large blooms
              Rayonnante 'White Tokyo'
              Yellow Rayonnante
          Fern green
          Gladioli, peach
          Old Man's Beard: Wild Clematis
          Pampas grass

layout the colleges have been established on virtually the same plan. Each is entered through a gatehouse in which a porter has a room where he deals with enquiries and sees who is entering and leaving. Many entrances are elaborate, like 'Tom Tower' at Christ Church, which was designed by Sir Christopher Wren.

The gatehouse of each college opens into the front quadrangle, which in most of the colleges conforms to the ancient plan and has a trim lawn enclosed on three sides by students' rooms, while on the fourth stand the hall and chapel.

At Christ Church, the largest of the colleges, Great (Tom) Quadrangle is in proportion with the aims of so eminent a founder as Cardinal Wolsey, and has an ornamental pool which reflects the surrounding buildings and the statue of Mercury in the centre.

The predominant importance as a whole can be clearly seen.

The chapel of Christ Church itself ranks as the cathedral, a distinction which must be unique, dating back to 1546 by order of King Henry VIII.

The Cathedral Church of Christ, stands on the site of a Saxon nunnery and Chapel founded by Saint Frideswide who died about 735. A priory of Augustinian canons was later established and it was they who began to build the present church in about the year 1160. The main walls, pillars and arches of the nave, choir and transepts were probably erected during the next twenty years. The spire, said to be the earliest in England, was added early in the thirteenth century, together with the Lady Chapel to which the remains of St Frideswide were removed in 1289.

North Mymms

For this autumn wedding wrought-iron pedestals standing well above eye level (always a point to remember when arranging flowers for functions where people are standing) were placed in front of the pillars alongside the lectern and pulpit in the parish church of Saint Mary, North Mymms, a beautiful thirteenth century church set in natural parkland. (Incidentally, this was the actual group seen on the television screen when morning service was televised from that church the same weekend).

A large group of flowers beside the pulpit, designed and selected to complement the bridesmaids' dresses for a September wedding in North Mymms Church. White, yellow, peach, orange and green are the predominant colours.

116

Frosts permitting, the material I chose could well be picked in October. However, this group was carefully planned in colour to tone with the material of the bridesmaids gowns in September.

A warm light apricot would best describe this silk material and I was not only able to obtain flowers lighter and darker but the exact shade by using Roses:

'Peace'
'Beauté'
'Sutters Gold'
'Helen Bettina'
'Helen Traubel'

and Dahlias:

'Jean Fairs'
'Gina Lombaert'
and others unnamed

My supporting flowers, ranging from cream to bronze and foliage were:

Nicotiana affinis, 'Daylight'
Gladioli
Amaranthus caudatus viridis, Green Love-lies bleeding
Solidago 'Early Gold'—Golden Rod
Helenium
Atriplex hortensis cupreata rubra
Cynara cardunculus: arthichoke
Bergenia

With two inch mesh wire netting crumpled up for support I made my highest point at the back of the group and the width with the golden rod, tobacco plant, helenium and atriplex. The Peace roses growing in their characteristic manner were cut very long in order to introduce the colour high up in the arrangement and from there falling in stages through the different heights of the dahlias to the H.T. roses, cardoon etc. at the base.

One of eight groups specially planned for the wedding, they picked up and toned with the material of the bridesmaids gowns most beautifully. If it had been a dull day, which would have necessitated artificial lighting, they would have shone, however, blazing heat and brilliant sun was meted out to us, which gave flowers and dresses alike a natural warm glow.

When asked to decorate a church for a wedding I treat the entire occasion as a whole. I always give careful consideration to predomi-

117

nant colours in the church, including walls, hangings, altar frontals and carpets and finally the colourings of the dresses and flowers to be carried by the bride and bridesmaids.

Some years ago while I was making plans for a wedding in a delightful country church in Hertfordshire, I realised that white in any form, either flowers or material, would be out of place, as the pulpit and altar rails in mellowed alabaster lead me to the conclusion that the bride should wear cream and gold and carry cream flowers. Leading on from there in the sequence of colour, the flower arrangements in the church ranged from deep cream to yellow and golds.

Now the arrangement illustrated opposite is entirely made up of flowers in shades of pink. The silk hangings behind the flowers are mellow old rose damask. The bridesmaids in dull blue were able to carry bouquets of mixed pink flowers, so tying up with the arrangements in the church to give an overall colour scheme.

The contents of this large pewter-coloured pottery bowl could be found in July and early August. The foliage which I have used is white beam, Sorbus aria, lime, stripped of its foliage leaving only the bracts and flowers, and cardoon, such a useful grey leaf. The seed head, a light soft green, to the right of the arrangement is angelica, a very interesting shape and texture. The flowers in blue pinks and yellow pinks are, of course, lupins and foxgloves, which can have an extended flowering period if the centre stem is cut early in the season, so allowing for the growth of the side shoots. Amongst the foxgloves are Digitalis lutea, the charming pale yellow one. Peach and apricot alstroemeria add to the general melée of pinks, Oriental poppies too, 'Suttons Art Shades', in the most delicious pinks and greys one could ever imagine, (these of course could be substituted by roses later on in the season) can be seen to the left and centre of the group. July flowering peonies, introduced in the left of the picture, can of course be cut and arranged after a deep drink in water but if they are specially wanted even four weeks later, which brings us into August, they can be cut in bud with just the smallest bit of colour showing, left perfectly dry, wrapped in cellophane and placed in a refrigerator at a temperature between 35° F and 40° F and then abandoned.

One to four weeks later they may be taken out, their stems re-cut and split and placed in warm water, where they will grow and develop for about forty-eight hours and be ready for inclusion in an arrangement.

Finally, in order to add just the pale blue pink and the pale salmon pink which I needed for correct balance, I used glass-house grown carnations and gladioli. This group, one of six in the church, looked really superb and lasted for five days without dropping a single petal.

A yellow-pink and blue-pink collection beside the altar for a midsummer wedding at North Mymms.

Contents: Alstroemeria   Lupins
    Angelica—seed head Peonies
    Cardoon   Poppies—'Suttons art Shades'
    Carnations   Rhododendron
    Foxgloves   Whitebeam
    Gladioli

Enthronement of the Bishop of St Albans, John B. Taylor, 14 June 1980

The Bishop's Throne

The arrangement (see colour plate 9) built from floor to about five feet in height was made by using a wooden construction with containers attached. Each filled with well soaked oasis covered over with very fine polythene and a layer of two inch mesh wire netting.

The colour scheme which I was asked to follow was yellow, white with lime green to complement the colours of the Bishop's cope and mitre. With the precautions already stated, the flowers and foliage lasted for ten days, having been topped up and sprayed with water daily.

Wooden construction about four feet high.

The very fine arrangement in the sanctuary, at John B. Taylor's enthronement, was also made on a wooden construction; Mrs Nancy Spinks of St Albans used only white flowers.

Contents: Astilbe   Peonies
          Carnations   Privet
          Fern   Single chrysanthemums
          Foxgloves   Solomons seal
          Hosta   Stock—white and cream

Memorial Services

One of two large pedestal arrangements placed by a pillar where the choir joins the round church, in The Temple. The flowers, foliage and dried seed heads were specially selected to give the feeling of age, and were arranged on 28 October 1971 for a service of rememberance and thanksgiving for the late Lord Trevethin and Oaksey, PC, DSO, TD, DCL, Lord Chief Justice, a Master of the Bench of the Inner Temple, President of Haileybury College and Chairman of the Governors, who died in his ninety-first year (see opposite for contents of arrangement).

The Temple Church: Lord Oaksey

One of the great treasures of London. The Temple Church lies to the West of the City and belongs to two of the four Inns of Court, namely the Inner Temple and the Middle Temple, thus it is the lawyers' private chapel (see colour plate 13).

Built in the eleven hundreds and consecrated in February 1185 the Round Church was built on the model of the Church of the Holy

The flowers and foliage include:

Alstroemeria, cream and yellow. (*1*)
Amaranthus: green. (*2*)
Angelica seed head. (*3*)
Berberis berries. (*4*)
Carnations: 'Apricot Marble'. (*5*)
Celery, yellowing leaves. (*6*)
Chrysanthemum: 'Harvest Moon', 'White Tokyo', 'Shantung'. (*7*)
Forsythia foliage, turned bronze. (*8*)
Gladioli, peach. (*9*)
Hydrangea green and whites. (*10*)
Variegated ivy. (*11*)
Viburnum tomentosum, berries and foliage. (*12*)
Wild artemesia seed heads. (*13*)
Wild Clematis (Old Man's Beard). (*14*)
Wild cow-parsnip seed heads: Heracleum. (*15*)

Sanctuary flowers, The Temple, City of London; a small group in a leaden urn on a finely reeded mahogany torchère. Cream, peach and apricot are the predominant colours of the flowers matching the big group.

124

Sepulchre and has withstood hundreds of years of change and miraculously escaped the Great Fire of 1666. The Choir, as the rest of the church is known, was added and completed in 1240.

The Temple takes its name from the crusading Order of Knights Templars, founded in 1118 to protect pilgrims on the road to the Holy City. Though fortunate to escape the damage of the Great Fire, the Church suffered terrible damage from enemy action on a night in May 1941. At the same time the East windows by Willement (1842) were shattered, and so the new and existing windows were designed on medieval lines by Carl Edwards. The centre window was presented by the Glaziers' Company whose arms occupy a prominent position. At the top of the centre light Christ is enthroned as Supreme Judge. Other subjects depicted are the Blitz on the City with St Paul's Cathedral amid the flames, and the Temple Church as it was before the war. Below are two knights on one horse, an early symbol of the Templars. The North window bears the device of the Middle Temple, the holy lamb and flag, together with the figures of Henry I and Stephen. The South window has the device of the Inner Temple, the winged horse Pegasus, together with the figures of Henry II and III.

The altar table, standing in front of the Sir Christopher Wren reredos, has been furnished with a handsome crimson frontal with a central design in gilt taken from an eighteenth century pattern. The silver cross candlesticks and vases, in general use are all memorials to recent Masters of the Temple or of the Bench. So much history is embodied in the architecture, brasses, tombs, music and furnishings, coupled with famous worshippers, choir masters and choristers, that the Temple Church has much to offer the visitor to London.

Haileybury and Imperial Service College Chapel: The Memorial Service for the Master, William Stewart M.C., M.A.

Before entering this imposing building, Haileybury Chapel, it is as well to first dwell for a moment on the history of this famous Public School for boys.

On the outskirts of Hertford Heath, between the county town of Hertford and Hoddesdon lie a group of buildings. In October 1805 the East India Company, saw this area as a perfect site to build a training college for its administrators. The designs of William Wilkins (who later designed the National Gallery) were accepted and the building was completed in 1809.

In·1858 The East India College came to an end and in 1862 the Public School which we have today was founded.

The original chapel was designed by Wilkins but in only a few years, as the popularity of the School grew it could no longer accommodate the growth in numbers and was then redesigned by Sir Arthur Blomfield. In 1936 further reconstruction was found to be necessary; this work under the direction of Sir Herbert Baker led to many changes. An apse was added behind the altar, the seating was reorganised and the whole decorated in cream with touches of gold. The apse is pierced by five small stained glass windows. The altar is of stone faced with lapis lazuli and embossed with decorations of gilded metal. In 1942 The Imperial Service College amalgamated with Haileybury.

The soft colouring of the stone, so clear and clean looking is of course a perfect foil for decoration throughout the year.

The flower arrangement featured (see colour plate 12) was a tribute to a great man—The Memorial Service in gratitude for the life and work of The Master—William Stewart, M.C., M.A.

The arrangement made in a copy of a Georgian wine cooler was planned on the colours of The Master's gown and hood, black and white.

The foliage I used was sanseveria, monstera, variegated ivy with the ethereal leaf of Caladium candidum. The forced white pear blossom, with the natural black stems gives the colour combination that was intended, black with white. Included in the arrangement was cherry blossom, Viburnum burkwoodii, alder with the black stems and previous years cones, larch, cornus, laurel with well polished leaves for the occasion, Salix daphnoides, a handsome and delightful pussy-willow, with very large silver catkins carried on shining maroon stems; a twig or two of forsythia completed the collection of flowering branches and foliage.

Now for the flowers, I used arum lilies, which are a good dense white, with another beautiful lily, lilium longiflorum, accompanied by one of the loveliest daffodils 'Mount Hood', which opens a very soft pale cream, fading, when fully out, to pure white. To give a little highlight of bright green I added Helleborus corsicus and Euphorbia charasius. The group though immense was carefully planned for colour and textures, with flowing lines and movement and dignity befitting the occasion.

Harvest

Harvest time is a really lovely season of the year. For Church decoration it brings to mind all the warm colours of autumn, the warm yellows, the reds and oranges, the russets and browns, the lush fruits, the ripening corn, the ripe grapes and the foliage of forest and garden tree turning colour, the dahlias and chrysanthemums. As some of the garden plants change colour and fade, then is the time to use them if for only a day or two such as I have shown in the arrangement in a dish for the church window sill, and the pitcher for table or floor.

On one occasion for the pulpit of St Mary's, North Mymms, which was made and carved in the Jacobean period, so as not to detract from the carving of 400 years ago, I used the simple bookmark design (see photograph below). Five lengths of green velvet on to which was attached each arrangement.

The materials used were helichrysum, grasses, grevillea, skeleton-ized magnolia leaves, achillea, artificial grapes and eleagnus leaves.

Each flower and leaf was mounted on fine silver wire. A pair of 18 gauge wires covered in gutta-percha formed a stiff frame on to which the preserved material was bound. Beginning at either end I bound each flower and leaf separately on to the frame in order to meet in the middle, keeping an eye on the shape and outline all the way, to give the finished design a rugged yet symmetrical appearance.

Bookmark design used to decorate Jacobean pulpit of St Mary's, North Mymms.

Autumn Berries and Foliage

Container: Earthenware pitcher thirteen inches. Made in the South of England.

Description: A wealth of colour can be found in berries and foliage from the garden in Autumn. (See opposite for contents).

This group arranged in the very narrow neck of the pitcher can be seen to be high on the handle side, with a flowing line coming from the lip and accentuating the fact that it is a jug. The fine arching stems, specially selected for this purpose, make it possible to arrange them in such a neck.

There are times when a tall, narrow necked vessel is the only shape that will either accommodate certain material or fit into a certain space.

Contents: 'Amaranthus caudatus viridis. (*1*)
Angelica. (*2*)
Berberis wilsonae. (*3*)
Cynara cardunculus or cardoon. (*4*)
Hosta fortunei. (*5*)
Hydrangea. (*6*)
Peony. (*7*)
Rhododendron. (*8*)
Vitis vinifera purpurea vine. (*9*)

The pitcher of soft sand colour has lead glazing at the neck of burnt ochre; this, with the collection of bold shapes, interesting colours and textures, makes a very handsome arrangement.

Autumn seed heads and foliage
Container: Serving dish

Description: In this autumn arrangement designed for a harvest window sill is a great variety of shapes, textures and colours; foliages, seed-heads, fruits and berries, grey, variegated, green, preserved, dried—in fact as much variety of material for the inspiration of the enthusiast to grow in his own garden. (See opposite for contents).

The fruit and gourds rest on the netting, while the living material passes through the wire netting support into the shallow water, which is quite sufficient for its needs for a day or two.

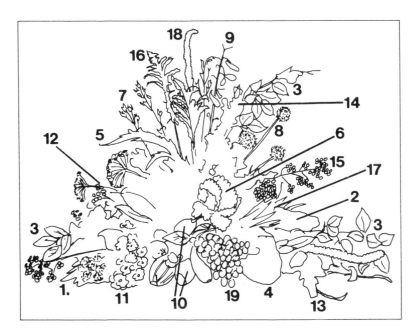

Contents: Azalea. (*1*)
Barley. (*2*)
Beech. (*3*)
Begonia rex: 'Iron Cross'. (*4*)
Cardoon. (*5*)
Decorative cabbage. (*6*)
Delphinium (Delphinium Larkspur). (*7*)
Echinops. (*8*)
Galtonia. (*9*)
Gourds. (*10*)
Hydrangea. (*11*)
Hypericum. (*12*)
Ivy. (*13*)
Nicandra (Apple of Peru). (*14*)
Privet. (*15*)
Solidago. (*16*)
Sweet corn. (*17*)
Verbascum. (*18*)
White grapes. (*19*)

Autumn arrangement of Korean Chrysanthemum, Berries and foliage

Container: Copper trough. Length 12 in./30 cm.

Contents: Amaranthus caudatus viridis
          Angelica
          Berberis wilsonae
          Cardoon: Cynara cardunculus
          Hydrangea
          Korean chrysanthemum, various:
             'Flame'
             'Gretel'
             'Primrose Day'
             'Wedding Sunshine'
          Peony
          Rhododendron
          Vitis vinifera purpurea

Description: A group of flowers, foliage and berries, arranged for a side table or window sill, ranging in colour from cream to terra cotta and copper to bronze.

Stage 1

Stage 2

Stage 3

A Porch Arrangement

A welcoming arrangement for the church porch of Saint Mary's, North Mymms, Hertfordshire. Standing beside the inner door on the one side and the board which records all the incumbents from the year 1237, the first named Thomas de Saint Albans right up to the present day. Flowing lines with autumnal colours for the harvest weekend.

Contents: Allium siculum   Fennel
           Carnations 'Harvest Moon'   Golden Rod
           Chrysanthemum   Hydrangea
           Eleagnus   Nicotiana, tobacco plant

Christmas

Gilt lantern to decorate the porch. Adults and children alike are lured by the attraction of candles. Gold, red, dark green and white make up the colours of this lantern of artificial flowers and foliage, Christmas roses, ivy holly and mistletoe.

Christmas—a colourful wreath for the church door. Fresh variegated holly leaves and eleagnus and natural pine cones arranged in five groups on a mossed wreath frame. Each leaf, cone and berry radiates from the centre of its own group. A good quality shining scarlet ribbon made into two bows for each group finishes off my design—with the addition of an extra important bow at the top with long tapering ends.

136

INDEX

(References to page numbers, with bold referring to colour plates)

140

Nepeta 'Six Hills', 22, 25
Nephrolepis todioides (Fern), 46
Nerine, 23
Nicandra physaloides (Shoo Fly Plant), 40, 44, 69, 71, 131
Nicotiana: 'Lime Green' (Tobacco Plant), 24, 65, 69, 74, 97, 117, 134
Nigella (Love-In-A-Mist, Hardy Annual), 40

Oak (Quercus), 9, 44
Oenothera (Evening Primrose), 40
Old Fashioned Pinks, 23
Old Man's Beard (Wild clematis; Travellers Joy), 38, 71, 113, 114, 123
Onion (Allium), 38
Onopordon (Thistle; Cotton thistle), 25, 41, 65, 101
Oregon Grape (Mahonia), 29
Oriental Poppies, 23
Osmunda regalis (Royal Fern), 37, 43

Pampas grass, 40, 41, 114
Papaver, 40
Parrotia persica, 28, 30, 48
Parsnip, Wild (Pastinaca sativa), 12, 36
Pear, 126
Penstemon, 22
Peony (Paeonia), 23, 40, 44, 60, 67, 119, 129
Peony (Herbaceous; Tree), 20, 40, 121, 129, 132
Peperomia magnoliaefolia variegata, 46
Periwinkle (Vinca), 65
Philadelphus, 17, 20, 60
Philadelphus coronarius aureus, 20, 24
Phlox, 65
Physalis (Cape gooseberry), 38
Physostegia virginiana, 22
Phytolacca, 97
Pieris, 27
Pine, 136
Pine Cones, 136
Pinks (Cottage Pinks; Dianthus), 23, 25
Plantain Lily: Hosta, 40, 63, 69, 73
Plume Poppy (Bocconia or Macleaya), 23, 41
Poinsettia, 80
Polyanthus, 23, 51, 58
Polygonatum multiflorum (Solomon's Seal), 69, 121
Poplar, Balsam, 48
Poppy, 17, 40

Poppy: Californian tree (Romneya coulteri)
    Oriental, 'Suttons Art Shades', 23, 60, 119
    Peony flowered, 73
Portugal Laurel, 27
Primrose, Evening (Oenothera), 40
Primrose (Primula), 102
Primula denticulatea, 23
Privet (Ligustrum), 24, 121, 131
Prunus avium, 126
Prunus: davidiana alba, 30, 34
    pissardii nigra, 30
    spinosa communis (Almond), 30
    spinosa (Wild plum), 52
    subhirtella autumnalis, 29
    subhirtella autumnalis rosea, 29, 30
    'Tai-Haku', 29
Pussy Willow (Salix), 28, 48, 126
Pyrethrum, 22
Pyrus salicifolia pendula (Willow leaf pear), 25, 34
Pyrus pear, 126

Quercus (Oak), 44
Quince, 30, 69

Ranunculus, 23
Raspberry leaves, 37, 43
Red Hot Poker (Kniphofia), 22, 60, 67
Rhodanthe, 71
Rhododendron, 27, 31, 44, 119, 129, 132
Robinia, 32
Romneya coulteri (Californian tree poppy), 21, 24, 65, 97
Roses, 10, 17, 18, 19, 20, 25, 36, 42, 60, 67, 71, 80, 101, **9**
Rose: 'Albertine', 63
    'Canarybird', 18
    'Cécile Brunner', 103
    'Colour Wonder', 74
    'Dr Van Fleet (New Dawn), 63
    'Gletcher', 73
    'Goldilocks', 63
    'Grandpa Dickson', 74
    'Beauté', 117
    'Helen Bettina', 117
    'Helen Traubel', 117
    'Iceberg', 111
    'Lavender Lassie', 73
    Miniature, 102
    Moss, 18
    'Pascali', 74
    'Peace', 69, 117
    'Roselandia', 109, 111

Willow Leaf Pear (Pyrus salicifolia pendula), 25
Willow (Pussy willow; Salix), 28, 48
Winter Jasmine (Jasminum nudiflorum), 28
Winter Sweet (Chimonanthus-praecox), 28, 50
Winter Sweet (Chimonanthus fragrans), 28
Wisteria, 20
Witch-Hazel (Hamamelis mollis), 28, 30, 48
Woad, 71
Wood Olive (Eleagnus), 27, 29, 44, 101, 127, 134

Xeranthemum (Everlasting), 41

Yarrow (Achillea), 38, 41, 70, 127
Yew, 9, 24
Yucca, 25

Zantedeschia aethiopica (Arum Lily), 11, 17, 57, 101, 126
Zea mays gracillima variegata (Sweet Corn; Maize), 39, 41, 71
Zinnia, 79